PRAISE FOR
The Lost Etheridge

"I can still hear Etheridge Knight's voice, saying his most well-known poems, in bars and college campuses during the years before his death.... To hear his voice again in this stunning collection is a precious gift. In all the poems, from the revolutionary / political poems in the sixties to the personal poems from the eighties, his passion, intelligence, and kindness are, as was often said of him, overwhelming. As is his commitment to his Holy Trinity — the poem, the poet, and the people. "I sing thee freedom," he writes in one of his final poems in this deeply moving collection, "For WE not one. I am done."

— Susan Neville, author of *The Town of Whispering Dolls*

"Norman Minnick has done a service to American poetry by assembling, in *The Lost Etheridge*, a trove of Knight's unpublished and out-of-print work: everything from relatively early wonders (as well as experiments and struggles), to profound prose meditations, to late masterpieces. ("O Elizabeth" alone is worth the price of the book). In between, Knight the great wit, the great love (and lust) poet, the verse philosopher, the vivisectionist of American hypocrisy, the Augustinian self-analyst, and the haiku master take their turns illuminating what Knight calls "the essential human / being."

— Michael S. Collins, author of *Understanding Etheridge Knight*

"There is an immediate sense of awe and gratitude in knowing a document like *The Lost Etheridge* exists. Pairing selected poems from his seminal collections with uncollected and unpublished works, this is the book we've hoped for: an invaluable testament to a poet who was / is equal parts South, Midwest, Black Arts, and unfettered imagination. 'But lusty and magic am I, magic is me,' the poet proclaims, and we hold the tome tighter, miss him even more."

— Mitchell L. H. Douglas, author of *dying in the scarecrow's arms*

"This collection is to be savored — an offering for the people of Knight's signature humor, plain-spoken truths, and musicality."

— Lydia Johnson, *The Indianapolis Review*

the lost etheridge

the lost etheridge

UNCOLLECTED POEMS
OF ETHERIDGE KNIGHT

EDITED BY
NORMAN MINNICK

FOREWORD BY
YUSEF KOMUNYAKAA

KINCHAFOONEE
CREEK PRESS ≈ ATHENS, GA

Copyright © 2022 by Kinchafoonee Creek Press. Editor's note copyright © 2022 by Norman Minnick. Foreword copyright © 2022 by Yusef Komunyakaa. All rights reserved.

ISBN: 978-1-7350172-8-0

Acknowledgments:
Poems have been selected from the following books: *Poems from Prison* (Broadside Press, Detroit, 1968); *Bellysong and Other Poems* (Broadside Press, Detroit, 1973); *Born of a Woman: New and Selected Poems* (Houghton Mifflin, Boston, 1980).

Other poems first appeared in the following publications: *Amaranthus* (For Huey P. Newton a Blk / Leader; The Nixon Flu; A Poem for Lincoln University), *American Poetry Review* (Haiku for the Homeless; On the Removal of the Fascist American Right from Power; Song of the Homeless; Three Haiku [O praying mantis], [I watch from afar], [The car accident]), *The Black Scholar* (Dearly / — Beloved / — Mizzee; Hip / Notes to My / Self), *The Café Review* (Blues for a Lady in Boston; [It is a bitch no break]; Warning), *Callaloo* (I Am a Tree, My Lovers Fly to and From Me; Junky's Song), *Elizabetheridge* (Betty Blues; Chance Dancer; O Elizabeth; Out of the Tunnel), *The Indianapolis Anthology* (Leaving Indiana after X-Mas, 1987), *The Iowa Review* (The Point of the Western Pen), *Milk Quarterly* (Hat Questionnaire), *Painted Bride Quarterly* (Memo #75; Things Awfully Quiet in America; Who Knows???).

Lend Me Your Ear first appeared in *The American Poetry Review*; On the Oral Nature of Poetry first appeared in *Painted Bride Quarterly* and reprinted in *The Black Scholar*; Preface to *Born of a Woman* first appeared in *Born of a Woman: New and Selected Poems* (Houghton Mifflin, Boston, 1980).

On Etheridge Knight by Modupe Labode first appeared in Indiana Humanities blog, April 27, 2016.

Special thanks to Elizabeth Gordon McKim, Etheridge Knight's literary executor, for permission to publish these works. Thanks also to Broadside Press for permission to reprint poems from *Poems from Prison* and *Bellysong and Other Poems*.

Cover photo © Indiana Historical Society. Frontispiece photo by Ellen Stack. Author photo by Elizabeth McKim. Designed by Norman Minnick.

www.kcpress.org

CONTENTS

Editor's Note   *xv*
Foreword   *xvii*

UNPUBLISHED POEMS (1964-1968)

I See No Single Thread	3
Johnny Mathis' Ruby	4
Ray Charles' Ruby	5
Convict Lust Fantasy	6
Vision	7
A Day in the Desert	8
Fresh Snow in Prison Yard	10
Convict's New Year's Eve Party	11
On the Way to Prison	12
Lately Feeling	14
Yellow Wood	15
Rufus	16

from POEMS FROM PRISON (1968)

To the Man Who Sidled up to Me and Asked: "How Long You in Fer, Buddy?"	21
To Make a Poem in Prison	22
Crazy Pigeon	23
Sweethearts in a Mulberry Tree	24
A Love Poem	25
On Universalism	26
A Nickel Bet	27

Beware:	28
For P.F.C. Joe Rogers	29
Peace	30
Portrait of Malcolm X	31
To Dinah Washington	32
To Gwendolyn Brooks	33

from BELLY SONG (1973)

Relaxing in the Charity Ward at Mercy Hospital	37
Huey	38
At Forty-four	39
Haiku 2	40
Dark Prophesy: I Sing of Shine	41
A Poem to be Recited	43
People Poem	44
After Watching B.B. King on T.V. While Locked in No. 8 Cell, No. 5 Cage of the Bridgeport, Conn., State Jail	45
Untitled 1	46
Untitled 2	47
Jazz Drummer	48
One Day We Shall All Go Back	49
Prison Graveyard	50
A Watts Mother Mourns While Boiling Beans	51
For Eric Dolphy	52
This Poem Is For	53
A Love Poem	54
The Last Poem	55
Notice	56

UNPUBLISHED POEMS (1968-1981)

Black Spring	59
Black Eyes	60
Fire Circled Rainbows	61
New Militant	62
Outlaw Sketch	63
Winter	64
Weird Town Anthem	65
Naked Boy	66
Chrysalis	67
Love Song	69
Lovely Terry	70
[Gush man picks]	71
To Mary Sleeping by Herself with Me Hungrily Watching	72
Hippie Girl	74
Memo #1	75
Memo #7	76
Spring Star Nectar	77
McCoy	78
The Incantation	80
Black Boy	81
Courage	83
The Other Side of the Wheel	84
Can I	87
Vietnam Is Harlem	88
The Isness and the Wasness	90
Truth	92
Faith	93
April 1975	94
First Week in June 1975	95
What Is Love	97
Staggering over the Bridge That John Berryman Jumped From	102

from BORN OF A WOMAN (1980)

From the Moment (or, Right / at — The Time)	105
Three Songs	107
For Dan Berrigan	110
Love Song to Idi Amin	111
A Poem for 3rd World Brothers	113
Welcome Home, Andrew Young — I'm / sho / glad that you didn't get Hung	115
Comes Now the Red Madness	116
A Conversation with Myself	117
The Ballad of Betty Dunn	119
Congressman Harold Ford	120
Looking at the Lake Where Otis Redding Lay	121
Lightnin' Hopkins Arrives in Detroit	122
A Shakespearean Sonnet: To a Woman Liberationist	123
A Personal Letter to Eldridge Cleaver	124

UNPUBLISHED POEMS (DATES UNKNOWN)

Curtains for Linesmen	129
Rejections	130
Losers	131
Winners	132
Unseen Definition	133
Fuck Now / Pay Later	134
At Delos	135
Prelude to a September Storm	136
Pin Pricks of Loneliness	137
Still Going Strong Blues	138
The Blue Duck	140
Bring It Home Blues	141
Parts	141

End of an Arm	144
Losses	146
No, I Can't Go to Jamaica This Year... I'm Goin to Jail Instead	147
I Try to Touch Your Grief	148
Jazz Haiku #2	149
Jazz Haiku #3	150
Sons of Thunder	151
Katie Lady — Won't You Please Come Home	152
A Poem for Our President: Whose Name, Ronald Reagan, Bears the Number of the Beast	153
Sharecropping Economics 101	154
Life?	155
Song to the Great Mother	156
Introduction	157
Turnpike Landscape	158
What We Make Of It	159
The Scholar Envious of His Neighbor	160
Four Views	161
New York City	162
The Reading Tour	163
I Remember Minnie	164
Prayers of a Prisoner	165
Waiting for Trial after Watts	166
Personal Property	167
[Coming to you]	168
Politics	169
Malcolm	170
Genocide	171
Iowa Dead	173
The Survivors	174
Terms	175
March in a Beanfield	176

UNCOLLECTED POEMS

The Point of the Western Pen	179
Things Awfully Quiet in America	180
On the Removal of the Fascist American Right from Power	182
The Nixon Flu	184
Who Knows???	185
Memo #75	187
Hip / Notes to My / Self	188
I Am a Tree, My Lovers Fly to and From Me	189
Dearly / — Beloved / — Mizzee	190
[It is a bitch no break]	191
Haiku for the Homeless	192
A Poem for Lincoln University	193
For Huey P. Newton a Blk / Leader	194
Song of the Homeless	195
Junky's Song	196
Leaving Indiana after X-Mas, 1987	197
Hat Questionnaire	198
Warning	200
Three Haiku	201
Blues for a Lady in Boston	202

UNPUBLISHED POEMS (1982-1991)

Freedom Chant for Blue Mt. Center	205
Your Song Ain't Really Blue	206
Some Days	207
Continuation Blues	208
Betty Blues	209
For Honey	210
The Fireman Speaks of Smoke Detectors	211

Walking the Streets of Memphis at 3 A.M., Dead / Broke and Stone / Sober	212
Poetfolio	213
Song of Br'er Mud-Turtle	215
[Somewhere in the free]	216
[If you want to find God]	217
A Mother's Day Poem, 1985	218
[Out of the tunnel into the Mississippi sun]	219
Mountain Mother	220
Ride, Sally Ride	221
For Jenifer McKim	222
She Comes to Me	223
Plea Poem	224
This Sun is Hot	225
The Hypocrite	226
Old Man Know-All	227
Revolutionaries Live in Houses of Love	228
After Listening to Ernesto Cardenal	230
E. S.	231
I Need for You to Tell Me	232
Deathrow	233
O Elizabeth	234
Chance Dancer	235
The Dance	236

PROSE

Preface to *Born of a Woman*	241
Lend Me Your Ear	243
On the Oral Nature of Poetry	249
On Etheridge Knight by Modupe Labode	258
Index of Poems and Prose	260

EDITOR'S NOTE

This volume collects over 200 poems from out-of-print books, literary journals, and those left in typescript and notebook form hidden away in university archives. *The Lost Etheridge* attempts to serve as a companion to *The Essential Etheridge*, an indispensable, albeit slim, volume of poetry published 35 years ago by University of Pittsburgh Press.

I was thrilled to discover an abundance of poems at The University of Toledo's Ward M. Canaday Center that were typed or neatly written and carefully preserved, especially since legend has it that Etheridge scammed the university by selling them nothing but newspaper clippings and telephone bills.

I am grateful to publisher Chris Jansen of Kinchafoonee Creek Press, whose dedication and conscientiousness enables brilliant works that would normally be overlooked to thrive; Elizabeth McKim, Etheridge's soul mate and literary executor whose stories, wisdom, advice, and abundant heart made this a marvelous and inspiring journey; Hanako Gavia, Etheredge's great-niece, for bestowing support and blessings on behalf of the family; Lynné Colbert at Mother Theresa Hackelmeier Memorial Library of Marian University for always being at the ready for a new challenge acquiring an obscure article or out-of-print book; and, of course, Sally Childs-Helton and Evan N. Miller at Irwin Library of Butler University, and Tamara Jones with the Ward M. Canaday Center at The University of Toledo.

Norman Minnick

FOREWORD

The collection of poems *The Lost Etheridge* edited by Norman Minnick seems perfectly timed. Etheridge Knight, the toastmaster — the man and the poet — is certainly hard to pin down. He would have been the first among us to stand up and say, "I'm not perfect." And at that moment the mask would have shifted slightly askance. Then, half-smiling, he would have said, "I wish I were a blues singer. Matter-of-fact, tonight I'm gonna sing for you 'Willow Weep for Me.'"

Here's a poet who possessed a genius for surviving the harsh realities of America. Having already read his poetry carefully for decades, I thought I knew an aspect of the man before I met him. He could've hailed from my hometown, Bogalusa, Louisiana. I'd written him once, in the early 1980s, from New Orleans to request poems about blues and jazz, and in response I received a handwritten letter from him that began with the endearment "Bro"; this was before I sought Sascha Feinstein's expertise on jazz and blues poems before we published *The Jazz Poetry Anthology*.

And years later, poet Kenneth May, my student at Indiana University in Bloomington, told me he was attending a late-night community poetry workshop with Etheridge at the Slippery Noodle Inn (a historical building that had been a stop along the Underground Railroad) in Indianapolis.

While some may see Etheridge as a trickster straight out of African American folklore or central-casting, decked out in his blue denim overalls, we could also rightfully say that he was an intellectual survivalist who knew the sharp turns of urban America. The man left a legend of stories behind him. Some takes were contradictory, but they were always intriguing, always filled with vim and vigor, with emotional sleight of hand, always disguised by a shim of innocence. It seems that sometimes Etheridge wanted to appear in contradiction, not wrestling with but embracing a duality: unlettered and wise, rural and urban, good and bad, or tough and sweet, cool and uncool. I remember saying that one could traverse the country and collect stories from poets as text for engaging biography. Consequently, Michael Collins' *Understanding Etheridge Knight* and Terrance Hayes' *To Float in the Space Between* are books that follow Etheridge's sojourns and collect stories about him into postmodern biographies.

I've heard numerous tales about Etheridge. In fact, Kenneth May says someone told him that Etheridge once sold his old car to someone, and then left town driving the car. I have heard some of the spoken-word poets portray Etheridge as the unlettered runagate badass, someone to emulate and imitate. I've been inclined to reprimand such portrayals while acknowledging within myself that any attempt at prettying-up his image would betray him. Indeed, he had come out the galleys of Southern folklore, and he even appropriated troublesome satire such as "Shine" as his own.

Etheridge loved reading books. I think books made him feel more complete, and maybe this is another thing he had in common with Malcolm X. I do know that he also at times attempted to disguise his love of intellectual pursuits. And in this sense, like Miles Davis, he seemed afraid that his intellectual currency would undermine his credit on the block. For the poet who's in the business of vamping on what he sees and feels, to ride roughshod on the brain can be a self-deceptive affair, and it is hard to believe that Etheridge wouldn't have known this in his gut.

In the late eighties, Kenneth May and I drove to Indy to meet a favorite poet. We visited Etheridge at his humble apartment. He seemed filled with energy: he was a natural-born storyteller, a poet who knew numerous poems by heart, and also a jailhouse toastmaster. I remember Sonny Bates holding on to Etheridge's every word. I also remember a reading he gave at Butler University; that evening he sang "Willow Weep for Me" and closed with Melissa Orion's poem "Where Is the Poet?" I remember him saying that he wished he had written the poem. I remember an entourage of his sitting in a small art gallery owned by Francis and Steve Stoller, and the place was buzzing with Etheridge's signifying.

A year or two later Etheridge was on his deathbed. Many poets and friends came from across the country to Indy to say their goodbyes. When Etheridge died, I broke a pact with myself. At eight years old, after my great-grandfather passed, I promised myself that I wouldn't attend another funeral, but I found myself that March day in 1991 at Crown Hill Cemetery trying to say goodbye to a poet whose work had touched me.

And it seems that poets are still saying their hellos and goodbyes. One disciple of the toastmaster is John Murillo, a poet who fully understands the scope of Etheridge's gift to us, which is self-evident as he pays homage walking Crown Hill in his long poem "Flowers for Etheridge" that opens with these lines: "I'm spending half this afternoon apologizing to ghosts, / Stepping over gravestones, the poet's Belly Song / In one hand, a ten dollar bouquet in the other." Now, as I talk to many young poets drawn to the core of Etheridge's down-to-earth life and art, to see them fully engaged and moved, as his voice insinuates beyond ordinary boundaries of time and place, I realize that this poet, this man, is still "poeting" for the twenty-first century, and *The Lost Etheridge* takes him further into tomorrow: this collection may make one feel the poet has been caught in the middle of working his signifying magic, making, and willing the spoken into the written, since he was known to bend time by reliving and teasing language into then and now, past and present.

In many ways, this compilation of uncollected poems and fragments that form *The Lost Etheridge* deepens our understanding of this poet and shows him to us intimately, in his own words, and what inherently emerges is a fuller portrait, the full thrust of his intellect and wit.

Yusef Komunyakaa

unpublished poems
(1964-1968)

I SEE NO SINGLE THREAD

I see no single thread
that binds me one to all;
even the common dead
each took the single fall.

No universal laws
or human misery
create a common cause
or common history
that ease my private pains
or break my private chains.

JOHNNY MATHIS' RUBY

Young and fragile, not yet ripe
But bursting with the promise of things to come
A girl running through a meadow of flowers
Elusive
Always just out of grasp

1965

RAY CHARLES' RUBY

Red and fiery and passionate
Trouble and pain
Love that scorches and then soothes
A full mature woman

1965

CONVICT LUST FANTASY

You'll look like a half-open jackknife
cause I'm gonna grab an uncover your
dibble drippin hungry for my angry
teeth. Gonna put it on the stove an
make it bubble and glow like hot lava.
Then I'll freeze it like a sweet strawberry.
I'll cover it, spit in it, and blow it
up like a plastic bomb. Baby it'll burn
like a forgotten fire poker and please
like a sugar wafer. You'll think it's
a snake wiggling till you scream daddy
stay home. Got to ride easy though
cause I gotta ride long.

January 1967

VISION

I live
in the eye
of coyotes.
We stare over
barren beauty
short cactus —
tough grass.
We weep
and turn to
deeper cover.

September 1967

A DAY IN THE DESERT

The heinous vulture
is held low against
the sky by willing
winds.
He sights his prey
like bees discover
pollen in the heart
of daisies smiling
brightly at the
magnificent wing.
The creature: Man
or beast, struggles
staring at the sun;
more beautiful behind
the noble span of
eagle outline.
The vulture looks
upon the sacrifice
of which its existence
depends.
He creeps downward
dragging heavy death.
The feast spots
the vulture's merciful
gift and smiles
baring teeth signaling
his readiness to receive....
Death drops free....

The patient bird
performs his grisly
function with delight;
deriving meaning.

October 1967

FRESH SNOW IN PRISON YARD

Exquisitely terrible
like the maiden
in a convict dream
who vanishes in chipped
paint of prison steel.

I see no snow, but old faces
that nullify all
cognizance save that of
rushing toward death,
recalling ghost icons
haunting fresh snow.

November 1967

CONVICT'S NEW YEAR'S EVE PARTY

This year, thirty minutes away,
is old like the vintage of a
fresh broken seal.
I have tended
its progress and tap'd its cask
searching for possibilities.
Now
with the year's death at hand,
a convict blows a happy horn
to announce the moment of departure.
Gone where?
Already it fades like a shadow
at dawn and I think I shall be freed
this year; yet I dare not rejoice,
for I have walked at this year's side
and I know not what of me has gone
with it.

January 1968

ON THE WAY TO PRISON

I looked into the
face of the sun.
I heard the sound
of automobiles.
I fell back into
childhood
among old toys
and little boys.

I returned and
relooked with recrimination
at the sun
who betrayed me;
his light and smile
feigning hope.
Repressor! Repressor!

The captors beside
me displayed no hate
only smug arrogance
empty as a nazi's soul.

I felt chains round
my waist,
cuffs round my
hands,
a crack round my

heart,
as black birds
of freedom spilled
out.

1968

LATELY FEELING

Hollow eyed like the moss
covered log in Alice's dream.
There is no wind.
The scent is heavy with the
subtle musk of parasitic growth,
and the silent bird perched
on the dead limb broods.
Its skeleton gleams in the
half moonlight while vermin
stalk vermin. There is
no other prey here; only the
dead and the vermin.

May 1968

YELLOW WOOD

Mother taught me.
I learned about despair when
I smiled instead of weeping
as she'd sit blue as the
heavy pot belly stove,
overcome with a promise tinted
futility;
angry as God
between her affair with sweep and scrub.

Needing laughter
she'd think of a stronger arm,
but seeing me:
a holy devil protested,
decently attacking
thin floors
that spun
undefeatable yellow.

Thinking quiet in my toy,
I watched
looking cool
for mother.

August 1968

RUFUS

(For Tom Govan, Dee Dee, Don, etc.)

Now there is no form
to slip into,
but there never was.
Goddam! I'll go to the
shadows
and make nothing of
images.
They are the statement
of meaning.

That fucking devil is
a dam.
Let me flood him; drown
him.

Hearing the soul over
burdened with voice.
Heavy blue voice:
bleeding from eternal
castration;
stirring the women;
Black women, White women
Goddam you!
Their thighs speak of my
function;
my assertion,
and my tears as they
wiggle out the door

smiling.

My violence
after the liquor ritual
the reefer smoke
curling...
I'll do tricks for the
children
or
go down the street to show
the other woman,
get her money
and cry
watching her wiggle out
the door smiling.

poems from prison
(1968)

TO THE MAN WHO SIDLED UP TO ME AND ASKED: "HOW LONG YOU IN FER, BUDDY?"

You need lightning
to strike
the circle of the moon
your teeth false
click nicely

you are
light bulb bright
and acey deucey tight

yours is the song
of massa
      so kissed
jest looking fer a home
jesus looking for a home

you need lightning
to strike
the circle of the moon
your eyes
sing
empty psalms

TO MAKE A POEM IN PRISON

It is hard
To make a poem in prison.
The air lends itself not
To the singer.
The seasons creep by unseen
And spark no fresh fires.

Soft words are rare, and drunk drunk
Against the clang of keys;
Wide eyes stare fat zeroes
And plead only for pity.

But pity is not for the poet;
Yet poems must be primed.
Here is not even sadness for singing,
Not even a beautiful rage rage,
No birds are winging. The air
Is empty of laughter. And love?
Why, love has flown,
Love has gone to glitten.

CRAZY PIGEON

Crazy pigeon strutting outside my cell —
Go strut on a branch or a steeple bell.
Why coo so softly in this concrete hell?

Fly away, dumb bird. Go winging off free.
Stop coo coo cooing, stop taunting me.
Find your pretty mate and let me be.

Like mine yours might be stone cold in her grave —
And mine too was pretty as a mourning dove.
Dumb prancing pigeon, mourning for your love.

SWEETHEARTS IN A MULBERRY TREE

I shinnied with Bea up a mulberry tree
When we were young and Arkansas was the world;
At sundown, among the leaves and worms,
We kissed, as bullbats swooped for gnats.

Beatrice now clicks down Sixty Third Street
In high and fire-red heels;
And in Arkansas, in the evenings,
The bullbats still catch gnats.

A LOVE POEM

I do not expect the spirit of Penelope
To be in your breast, for I am not mighty.
Or fearless (only our love is brave,
A rock against the wind.) I cry and cringe
When the cyclops peer into my cave each hour
On the hour.

I do not expect your letters to be lengthy
And of love, flowery and philosophic, for
Words are not your love, nor our bond.
I need only the hard fact
Of your existence for my subsistence.
(Our love is a rock against the wind,
Not soft like silk and lace.)

ON UNIVERSALISM

I see no single thread
That binds me one to all;
Why even common dead
Men took the single fall.

No universal laws
Of human misery
Create a common cause
Or common history
That ease black people's pains
Nor break black people's chains.

[This is a revision of an earlier poem, "I See No Single Thread"]

A NICKEL BET

Be slow. Fold the daily news
Carefully. There is yet
One more section to peruse

And one more station till your stop.
Now, slowly turn the page, let
Your finger trace across the top.

Again your number did not fall,
But for a day the nickel bet
Made your hopes ten feet tall.

BEWARE:

The Mississippi cop,
The Plague, the Klan
And the card-tossing cat
Who's the flim flam man.

FOR P.F.C. JOE ROGERS

(killed at Inchon)

Now the moon mocks full and naughty,
Now winks behind a daisy cloud,
As the sea so cold and haughty
Serves as Joe Roger's shroud.

The clouds beyond the mountains rise
And catch the mortar's flashing light.
The wind is laced with aching cries:
There is blood on that moon tonight.

PEACE

Hound dog sits his tail
On the bank of long dark stream
And howls at the moon.

Rabbit sits in hole
On the hill and strokes his fur
In myopic fear.

Ringtail coon rests on
Log in stream, and grins, and waits
Till moon behind dog.

PORTRAIT OF MALCOLM X

(For Charles Baker)

He has the sign
of the time shining
in his eyes   the high sign

His throat moans
Moses on Sinai and cracks
stones

His lips lay full and flowered
by the breast of Mother Africa

His forehead is red
and sacrosanct and
smooth as time and
love for you

TO DINAH WASHINGTON

I have heard your voice floating, royal and real,
Across the dusky neighborhoods,
And the eyes of old men grow bright, remembering;
Children stop their play to listen,
Remembering — though they have never heard you before,
You are familiar to them:
Queen of the Blues, singing an eternal song.

In the scarred booths of Forty-Third street,
"Long Johns" suck in their bellies,
On the brass studded leather of Elite-town,
Silk-suited Bucks raise their chins…

Wherever a man is without a warm woman,
Or a woman without her muscled man,
The eternal song is sung.

Some say you're sleeping,
But I say you're singing.

Unforgettable Queen.

TO GWENDOLYN BROOKS

O Courier on Pegasus. O Daughter of Parnassus!
O Splendid woman of purple stich.

When beaten and blue, despairingly we sink
Within obfuscating mire,
Oh, cradle in your bosom us, hum your lullabies
And soothe our souls with kisses of verse
That stir us on to search for light.

O Mother of the world. Effulgent lover of the Sun!
Forever speak the truth.

belly song
(1973)

RELAXING IN THE CHARITY WARD
AT MERCY HOSPITAL

All the old / men
                lie dying
squirming in their own shit
in the Hospital named Mercy

All the old / men
                lie dying
                all day dying
                in the morning dying

When the well / fed / pink cheeked priest
at break of day follows a white / starched nun
thru the Charity / Welfare ward at the Hospital
named Mercy. The fat well fed priest
B
l
e
ss all the old / men who
                            lie dying
squirming in their own shit

HUEY

Wel / come back, brother
from...
the House of many Slams
to
these mean bricks

a poet
sung to me:
lets us
drink wine in the alley
and dance in the streets

everyday people
have found
a prince

bright-eyed
wonder-child

comes
Revolution.

AT FORTY-FOUR

At forty-four years of age
My dancing pa was dead.
"Just went to sleep," my mother cried.
"Peaked out," the doctor said.

HAIKU 2

1

Outside, the thunder
Shakes the prison walls; inside
My heart shakes my ears.

2

(For Sonia)

Snow from the mountains
Of my heart instantly melts
In your warm Blackness.

3

Black men with Torches
Follow the bloody tracks of
The albino beast.

4

Gray jets drag white tails
Across blue skies; gray rats drag
Tails across black legs.

DARK PROPHESY: I SING OF SHINE

And, yeah, brothers,
while white / america sings about the unsink
able molly brown
(who was hustling the titanic
when it went down)
I sing to thee of Shine
the stoker who was hip
enough to flee the fucking ship
and let the white folks drown
with screams on their lips
(jumped his black ass into the dark sea, Shine did,
broke free from the straining steel).
Yeah, I sing of Shine
and how the millionaire banker stood on the deck
and pulled from his pocket a million dollar check
saying Shine Shine save poor me
and I'll give you all the money a black boy needs —
how Shine looked at the money and then at the sea
and said jump in muthafucka and swim like me —
And Shine swam on — Shine swam on —
how the banker's daughter ran naked on the deck
with her pink tits trembling and her pants roun her neck
screaming Shine Shine save poor me
and I'll give you all the cunt a black boy needs —
how Shine said now cunt is good and that's no jive
but you got to swim not fuck to stay alive —
And Shine swam on — Shine swam on —
how Shine swam past a preacher afloat on a board

crying save me nigger Shine in the name of the Lord —
how the preacher grabbed Shine's arm and broke his stroke —
how Shine pulled his shank and cut the preacher's throat —
And Shine swam on — Shine swam on —
And when the news hit shore that the titanic had sunk
Shine was up in Harlem damn near drunk —
and dancing in the streets.
Yeah, damn near drunk and dancing in the streets.

A POEM TO BE RECITED

A poem
to be recited
while waiting in line to sign / up for your unemployment check
or
while standing in line to be fed in the prison mess-hall
or
while boarding a troop / ship for Vietnam
or
while walking thru the playground in "the projects:"

The Children in Blk america grow up quickly
(and they die young.
The Children in Blk america grow up quickly
(and they die young.

The Children in Blk america have sad eyes.
The Children in Blk america have sad eyes.
The Children of Blk america are ashamed of their fathers.
The Children of Blk america are ashamed of their fathers.

PEOPLE POEM

(For Patrice Lumumba)

they ripped him off
yes they did

all of his kingdoms
all of his castles
all of his empires
all of his dreams

they ripped him off
yes they did
they ripped him off
yes they did

AFTER WATCHING B. B. KING ON T.V. WHILE LOCKED IN NO. 8 CELL NO. 5 CAGE OF THE BRIDGEPORT, CONNECTICUT, STATE JAIL

And now man
as you stand there
in the white glare
the sound I hear
from your tuxedoed frame
somehow ain't the same
that's filled my belly and ears
for so many many years
yet the pain on your face is the same
despite the gloss and the glitter and the fame
and the new name:
CULTURE
and now man
with the sound
of your songs ringing round
these bars in sad procession
I think of a sonia / poem:
"Blues ain't culture —
they sounds of oppression —
of the game the man's been running
all these years."

UNTITLED 1

    1

Before you
my days had two lean faces.
I stripped them bare and stacked
them in the south corner of my mind.
Back to back they stood —
like hostile lovers

    2

For Third World Guerrillas, urban or otherwise:

Men who move in mountains
are the first to see the sun,
are the last to see it leave.
Here in the valleys we live in shadows,
here light does not linger late —
early night hides the slender self....

UNTITLED 2

Death seeks first
the fire and earth.
Water and air
always die last.
Lions and Tigers
are doomed at birth.
Eels and sparrows
bloom forth
in the U.S.A.

JAZZ DRUMMER

MAX ROACH
        has fire and steel in his hands,
        rides high, is a Makabele warrior,
        tastes death on his lips, beats babies
        from worn out wombs,
                              grins with grace,
        and cries in the middle of his eyes.

MAX ROACH
        thumps the big circle in bare feet,
        opens wide the big arms,
        and like the sea
                calls us all.

ONE DAY WE SHALL ALL GO BACK

(For Jake & Margaret Milliones, and Nicky & Curtis)

One day we shall all go back —
we shall all go back (down home
to the brown hills and red gullies (down home
where the blood of our fathers
has fed the black earth (down home
where the slow / flowing rivers, dark and silent,
sing to the bones of our brothers (down home
wrapped forever in black wetness (down home....

One day we shall all go back (down home
we shall leave the cold northlands
of icy stares, frozen hearts, stiff snot, cold flats,
racking coughs, hard cash, and go back (down home
to be kissed by sweet rain and warm sun on black backs.

We shall all go back (down home
to avenge Medgar, and Martin, and lil Emmett Till,
and all the others who died the good death (down home —
back — back to avenge our fathers and mothers killed and raped
in Natchez, Memphis, Montgomery, Mobile, Lake Charles,
New Orleans, Baton Rouge, Macon, Waycross, Charleston,
Jackson, Savannah, Tougoloosa....

One day we shall all go back —
We shall surely all go back (down home
and the southland will tremble to our marching feet (down home
where our freedom cries will shake the southern skies (down home
and the shame will leave our children's eyes (down home....

PRISON GRAVEYARD

The dying sun
slides over the tiger teeth
lying row on row
beneath the high and western wall.

And tonight as the keepers
march in the moonlight
the spirits will rise and fret

And fight because no hymns
were sung to soothe
them on their journey
no mourners have stood
and wept;

So the spirits dance
the devil's step, and are kept
from riding the winds to the sea.

A WATTS MOTHER MOURNS WHILE BOILING BEANS

The blooming flower of my life is roaming
in the night, and I think surely
that never since he was born
have I been free from fright.
My boy is bold, and his blood
grows quickly hot / even now
he could be crawling in the street
bleeding out his life, likely as not.
Come home, my bold and restless son. — Stop
my heart's yearning! But I must quit
this thinking — my husband is coming
and the beans are burning.

FOR ERIC DOLPHY

on flute
spinning   spinning   spinning
love
thru / out
the universe

i
know
exactly
whut chew mean
man

you like
tittee
my sister
who never expressed LOVE
in words (like the white folks always   d
she would sit in the corner   o
and cry   i
everytime   n
i   g
got a whuppin

THIS POEM IS FOR

NEW YORK CITY
With its 8 million People
Who stand and watch, silently,
A Sister or Brother (Black or White or Yellow or Red)
Being
Raped or robbed —
A Poem for NEW YORK CITY
And for
The Junkies of 115th and Lenox Avenue, for
Madison Avenue jr. executives, for
old ladies and men, with their dogs,
shitting on curbs;
        i pee
        on thee. (period)

                — Etheridge Knight Soa

A LOVE POEM

And Mary / is / on the High / Way
coming to me / thru the rain
And the wind.
And.
We are Singing.

       — Etheridge Knight Soa
         Jeff / City, Mo. —
         Sept. 1, 1972

THE LAST POEM

(that'll be coming at you, thisaway)

'Pears to me   that

WE
Whatever bag we be coming out of
Have
Been
Bullshitting... (cepting the Messenger, of course)

Maybe — just maybe...
Poet.

— Etheridge Knight Soa

NOTICE

The
7 Sons Seven
Suns
)
   7)
of Africa

      — Etheridge Knight Soa

unpublished poems
(1968-1981)

BLACK SPRING

Flowers are growing
out of wine bottles:
the little children
are fresh from heaven
to do some vital
cleaning.
God knows they have
a job.
So do we.

December 1968

BLACK EYES

Surrounded by
wrinkled velvet
are wet tales
of resentment
smoking up the
stomach.
A blood line
gash
smiles and smiles
that does not
disguise the
ice hot murder
within.

December 1968

FIRE CIRCLED RAINBOWS

Dream Dream fairy frog.
What are we to flower
petal so pale in the
sunshine?
Bear claws, puma paws.
On a plate glass heart
elves are drowning in
our weeping pools.
Those who lie, burn my
magic.

1969

NEW MILITANT

I froze my feet
parking cars
on New Year's Eve.
The white ladies
were dressed so fine.
Something in me
snapped.

January 1969

OUTLAW SKETCH

Sometimes I rode side
sharp panthers
in yellow trousers and
leather vests.
At night
we stalked the city
discovering nothing
except the plunder
rumbling through our
starving feet.
Our hardness was
silence in police stations
where at night abandoned
children with comely
black mothers
pushed through dreams
insulated with marijuana.
Still
we moved through the
streets light as dancers;
as if something beautiful
was in the air.

January 1969

WINTER

When I'm stoned
in biting blue
morning air;
car starters
sound like monkey
battles.
When the motor
starts I feel warm
wrapped wholly snug
in the rumble rumble.

January 1969

WEIRD TOWN ANTHEM

Oh blood! blood!
why thicken
why rush
why make my
stomach sick:
coils like an
ugly steel spring,
springing nothing!
Revulsion!
Revulsion!
Soft clinging mush
neutralizes my
insipid innards.
Oh woe!
I must have dope
to hold my innards
together.

January 1969

[NAKED BOY]

Naked boy
flopping like angel wings
listen to the wind sing.
Deep, deep under the
quietest clover
lay secrets round as
Roman women in piles
close as grape clusters.
Oh dance with he whose
pointed ears
cast suggestions like
flowing ribbons of flowers
rippling in waves through
her breath.
The gentle caress speaks of
the unutterable gifts
Solomon lost in his
drunken dreams.

1969

CHRYSALIS

I was a 17 year old man
when Aunt Mae died.
Cool as morning earth
I said: "Gee, when is
the funeral?"
        If she could
        see me now...
        This man...
I carried her coffin
box with the men; who
appeared more proud on
this occasion.
I rode straight up in
the negligible dignity
of a big Cadillac.
        I'm a warrior performing
        the death ritual.

At the grave, I stood
tall as Indians I had
seen idling outside
South Dakota taverns.
My pride soared like the
little sparrow
making curious swoops
over the gathering.
Meaningless words were
spoken

and people began to leave.
I stayed; watching workmen
pick up shovels.
The pebbles plinked against
the steel,
making empty sounds that
cracked my manhood wide
open
like the split head of
a foolish john found dead
in the alley on Sunday
morning.
Mt last piece of childhood
fell out in an uncontrollable
sob.
Melted into terrible tears.
I saw all I thought I
knew
buried under the dirt of Aunt
Mae's gravehole.
Now it's all over...
I'm a child for life.

March 1969

LOVE SONG

(For Terry)

Beside the petals
of the palest blue,
your face hides
among the velvet
green leaves shining
on spring mornings.

Beside the tuft
of the softest cloud,
your eyes challenge
the sun
inspiring dreams
akin to those
of the maddest man
or the loveliest child.

May 1969

LOVELY TERRY

A brown elf
whose skin is
of the softest
velvet
whispered quiet
secrets into
my ear:
the enchanted
whisperings of
magic have left
me mad with
delight.

May 1969

[GUSH MAN PICKS]

Gush man picks
up a bag of shining
stones.
He pours them like
wet diamonds in the
night
into urns ancient
as the smiles of tired
lovers.
      oh magic man sparkle
      oh magic man shine
poof like a dragon the
poet explodes.

June 1969

TO MARY SLEEPING BY HERSELF WITH ME HUNGRILY WATCHING

As you lie sleeping
I dream of a wild flower
clutching me as though
it were the mad eye'd
creature Adam discovered
smiling beneath the
fragrant trees.

I watch you sleep
nodding my head to the
soft rhythms of your breath.
My feet pat the floor
listening quietly to the
pathetic whisperings my
toes say to the thin
cheap carpet.

Alone you lie
as though you had time to bide
as though you had love to hide
as though men never died.

As you sleep
I see a jewel hidden
by a madman in the
darkness of a golden box.

As you sleep
dry tears shake through
the wisdom of my loins
who understand need beyond
me who understands nothing.

In the dream forest I
shudder with the flower
unable to bloom in
the sweetest spring.

Mary Mary
as you sleep
dry tears turn to dust
and lush forest dreams to
desert.

August 1969

HIPPIE GIRL

(For Runaway Susan)

Young pirates living
beside rivers
like cowboys
smile knowingly,
though fourteen years
have not shattered
the energy.
What brave children:
evading uncomprehending
police
and learning the things
bitter rats know.

October 1969

MEMO #1

i / git ass tired,
bone tired,
stone tired,
of everybody, including
me, always *telling*
blk / people what
blk / people *got* to do;
blk / people ain't *got* to do
a *damn* / thing
but
stay black, and die.

MEMO #7

no blood
is to kill
(or bad / rap)
another blood until
he has killed
a germ first.
(now watch the population
rise!)

1976

SPRING STAR NECTAR

overgrown weeds
sleeping pigs in broken down shed
the stars out over the creek
so many & bright

everyone else has gone

a wrinkled pink vein
up the stem of a weed
                          pulses

white clusters fold out
at the top

sweetness of whiskey & starlight
walking back up the hill of wild flowers
to sleep on the floor
in the few hours til morning

(the water bugs & spiders
put up a fight to keep it to themselves)

restless,
I turn toward the window
peeling white paint surrounds the black rectangles
splattered with bright white stars

June 12, 1976

McCOY

(For McCoy Tyner)

not necromancy
nor the manual alphabet

can account
for this alchemy

of divining spirits
                 &
                    communicating to the
                                     blind
which at one time accounts for us all

marjoram spread on the tautly stretched
        tympanum
                of
                        our
                            inner need

sitting high above the elaborate theatre
the percussion set on the stage in a range of color
                  & to me bizarre & beautiful shapes
& the men themselves in varied size, contour & expression of face,
body & instruments
                held holistically
                          each
                                  necessarily
                                            together

    & like a balcony god, for only $4.50, seeing the
                            universe of this creation,
                            this alchemical, musical world
                            this
                                        people
                                              world
                            spread below me, smiling on it
tho I had nothing to do with it
                except in reception
                          wch tho also important

shd not be overestimated, supplicatingly I left the upper realms to take an empty seat in the 4th row, to see them closer in the flesh, the range of Franco the percussionist's facial music, the intensity emanating from the leader McCoy into his piano & into his
    players

at this 6.50 range I was also transformed & I realized that god-like music is all around me, regardless of money & solitude

Easter, 1976

THE INCANTATION

she was tall
had tiny bits of mustache
on her upper lip

wore a short jean skirt
over heavy thighs

an ovaloid face looking younger still
than her 30 years
thin on top, an athletic t-shirt
of green & yellow v-front through
the deep brown of her skin

she had a clear strong voice
bordering on deep, clear eyes
attenuated on my words in the warm
air like mosquitoes trying to land

a magic, the stream brushing over rocks
next to us, children playing, adults
playing pic-nic, little paper cups,
constant trips to the keg, brushing off the
bugs as we grin at each other & talk

a magic soon remembered as the alchemy
of early evening in the beginning of
summer out of the city, remembering what
it's like to circle a woman, looking for
warmth

May 22, 1976

BLACK BOY

(For Smilie)

Pig pie
blood pie:
a smiling young Black
sharp in his leather
coat
stands in the street
with his shades on.

Hustling.

A pig pie
fresh and young
for pig obscenity
in a cell
in a college
in a factory.

Fresh and young
for pigs to kill
in alleys
crumbling in flames
of freedom
in wars retching
of depravity.

Pig pie
when pigs
live:

expect to die.
Pigs kill us
for being
the discrepancy.
Pigs kill to forget.

July 1970

COURAGE

I saw Crazy Horse's
great vision
counting coup
down Franklin Ave.

drunk;

smiling at people
and
joking with children.

Down that ugly street
he staggered.

A death chant under his
breath
prepared for resurrection

beside great spirits
and a brave warrior's
rage.

August 1970

THE OTHER SIDE OF THE WHEEL

To everything — turn — turn — turn;
There is a reason — turn — turn — turn;
There is a reason.
Like for say the new black man, yes, let's
talk about the new black man —
he no follow in footsteps of white definitions,
he no follow in footsteps of white interpretations,
he no follow in footsteps of white ethics,
he no follow in footsteps of white aesthetics —
yes everything turns, it keeps on turning.
White boys just don't turn fast enough.
They want to be friends with the oppressed, and
the oppressor at the same time.
They want to support and tear down those same
institutions at the same time.
They want to pray with niggers, eat with niggers,
sleep with niggers; do all those things with niggers,
except realize that the ex-nigger is now the new
black man; and the new black man only needs
the white man to keep the momentum going —
and to hell with the prayers,
to hell with the community meals,
to hell with the white woman's sexual hang-ups —
yes everything turns, it keeps on turning.
It is a spirit that was here in the beginning. It
was here, but we could not see it because it was
on the other side of the wheel, but the wheel
turns — it whirls — it rotates — it keeps going

round and round.
It finds black people saying to the police — "you have
to bring ass to get ass."
It finds black educators saying to little black children —
"the institutions of education are racist, and must be
burnt to the ground."
It finds black theologians speaking to the Capitalist
telling them — "capitalism is the chief anti-christ."
Yes everything turns, it keeps on turning.
And as it swirls it crushes the hearts of most
white people. It's making them say — "what do
those niggers want?" It's forcing them to dig down
deep into their paternalistic bags, and come up
with — "they're like little children, they aren't full
grown yet, they've been denied their history, and
stripped of their dignity." The wind from this whirl
is turning young white daughters and sons against
their mothers and fathers. It is forcing the Christians
to suffocate in their own piss and bowel movements.
It has allowed the elect to see Nixon as a pimp
and the statue of liberty as a prostitute. Someday
near indeed it's going to bless the poor, it's going
to liberate the oppressed, it's going to release the
captives — and it won't be pie in the sky.
When that time is at hand you'll know it
because whites won't be allowed into black ghettos,
black folks won't be picking any cotton,
children won't be bussed any longer,
the racist will be beat to death by their
legs pulled off,
the oppressor and their supporters will be made
to eat the flesh of each other, then drown
in their own vomit; but the most vivid

indication of this time will be the unity
of all black people, and they'll be singing
in three-part harmony —
To everything — turn — turn — turn;
There is a reason — turn — turn — turn.

CAN I

    take off my garments and expose
to you my naked soul?
    would you stare?
    would you gaze upon my meek
vulnerability, and laugh?
    would you distort and flex
myself into your petty little
world; or would you appreciate
the simplicity of my nudity?
    can I poet to you baby?
    can I poet, poet, poet?
eeeeeee iy iy iy iy iy iy ee
    can I talk about good folks?
America America — set me free
    don't gaze upon my naked soul,
set me free
    don't write me anymore poems —
set me free
    don't plunge at my vulnerability —
    By the way there's a revolution
going on will you come. I'll wait
awhile if you need time to shoot
your horse —
                — can I

VIETNAM IS HARLEM

Pieces of bones
blend well with the blood
that stink the air with pubic hair,
he's right how he's right,
he's ending the fight;

      and Harlem wasn't built overnight.

They being too,
like breath in a tube
originally in the scene of order,
but we call the orderer that delivers the shout —
move slow;

      Harlem wasn't built overnight.

Raising a child
to be a good boy
is contradictory to our philosophy;
rape up a hoe,
and cut up a preacher —
did you say that the fittest survive?
At least let's be real,
to hell with a pill.
I don't need chemicals to tell me;
give me a gun,
yes killing is fun,
move slow;

    Harlem wasn't built overnight.

It's a capitalist world,
and a capitalist war,
why are the social choiced so easy to fool;
cutting your uterus,
and carving your balls;
then forcing your hands to applaud;
but time will revenge,
the killing of our friends,
and robbing the ground of its oil;
and slowly he'll die,
Predestined
not I,
and late at night you'll hear his ghost say —
move slow;

    Harlem wasn't built overnight.

THE ISNESS AND THE WASNESS

If the isness is the wasness,
and the wasness is the isness,
then the isness must be mad at my pap;
at my pap
at my pap
at my sad black pap —

    and the niggers going to get you Mr. Man.

And to speak about a house,
and a house is not a home,
and the rats and the roaches share the crumbs.
Share the crumbs,
eat the flesh,
drink the blood,
vomit guts —

    and the niggers going to get you Mr. Man.

Tis the heart and it's sad,
fists are clenched, lips are mad,
and the militants have a field day with the brain;
and the colored folks like the Negro
Seek Survive
Seek Survive —

    and the niggers going to get you Mr. Man.

There's the pot, pan, and tub
like illusions faking love,
and the mothers marry yellow streaks of three;
If there's God up above
forget the stars
forget the sun —

  and the niggers going to get you Mr. Man.

Hear me cry, cheated pride,
and they tell me we are dumb
like the cow bruised her tits on the moon;
suck the guts,
clean the privates,
vomit stinks,
so does poor —

  and the niggers going to get you Mr. Man.

Day is gone, life is long,
and no bed to lay my head
and they want to use a penis for a test,
working hard, slumber deep
limbs are limp, slumber sleep —

  and the niggers going to get you Mr. Man.

If the isness is the wasness
and the wasness is the isness
then the isness must be mad at The Man;
at the man
at the man
at the sick, sad man —

  and my daddy really loved me all the time!

TRUTH

    is that which hurts the human self more than all. This is so because it challenges and forces the individual to reconsider what was previously taken for granted about who he is,
    is that which liberates the individual both body and soul, and leaves him a slave only to liberation,
    is that which leaves the individual lusting for more of it, because its satisfying, gratifying composition is that which allows the individual to experience the greatest amount of humanity,
    is a friend of the poor, oppressed, downtrodden, sick and lowly; cause it looks the oppressor in the face, and won't remove its haunting stare until death do them part.

FAITH

Struggle with it,
allow it to evolve, shift, distort.
Use any and all means necessary for
its survival. Guard it as if it's
the essence of you. Above all
things, know that its existence is
your existence, and its death is
your death.

APRIL 1975

I.

I was thinking of you
Again locks of your hair
Were twisted in the music
Like wood knotted against the pain

II.

I keep asking
The birds from the south
If the world is really
Starting all over again
Will the waves roll
The bloody feet off the shore?

III.

The chair across the room is empty
Next to it is a pile of hands
In the bright air
They fly around the room
Waving at someone I don't see

FIRST WEEK IN JUNE 1975

The Farm

I opened the door
Two flowers grew in the middle of the floor
I opened the window
The door blew off

I turned on the water
Rain fell on one side of the barn
I went to bed, alone
A hand lay at my feet

The River

He showed me the river
Put me into a canoe
And pushed me away from the shore
I could do nothing but fly

A hawk and an egret
Threw branches at the sun
Weeds threw out their arms
Begging me to take their children

Late afternoon
The river took up its bed
And walked.

The Dog

The Dog wore
A crown of ragweed
Its ears were pierced with time
But it smiled at my tears

The Dog can be a bed
 It carries a load of dirt and ticks
Its feet are like moccasins
I want to ride it home

The Boy

He came out of the woods
He came out of the kitchen
At his sister's call
He had white bird feathers in his hair

He never looked at me
But stared at the river
Stared at the sun
He gave me his hand
To put at the foot of my bed.

WHAT IS LOVE

(For Gregory Stephen,
the deep-sea diver, Green Beret, man of TALK)

1

One Maytime the dogwood
was it always this way
opened like thousands of
Chinese hands.
My street
a circle of
silent clap clap clapping

That might
have been the same
lovely Maytime
in a rice paddy
you shot
the dying woman
whose gut opened
like Hell's rose
and the blood
your blood, my love.

Oh, God,
my green man.
there's no God
but love.

In our torment

of night talk
long distance
the wires
go snap snap snapping
through the heart
the tremors
of war
like dogwood
like God's wood
words
words
I am mad
in fear of blossoming
to death.
You did. You did

with her
with all
with every round
with every flower burst
and bullet fall.

And is that why
you're not afraid
to die? And is that why

you make me love you?

    2

Vigilant
in an empty house

I count
the barren limbs
of black pine
cutting death down
to a nude yard,
and listen

rain beats
gunfire on
a grass hut

I sweep my sons' rooms clean

and fall
like a poor maid
through a trap door
to a princess world
of seagardens,
dream anemones,
your flagrant corals,
promises
changing life
one foot South
torso North
I break like a China doll,
from between the legs, up
up through belly, breast,
to the temple, a fine
hairline crack in the yell-
ow dream of life whole.

3

Up North
we sleep to Mozart
in gold-rimmed glasses.
I am aging.

You, so young,
helicopter out of
jungle rot and napalm
every night, and every night

and every night

you come to me with leeches					and love
you come to me with rifles					and love
you come to me with mud pits,
stale boots, ghost eyes,					love,
you come to me with lead					and love
mouths, baby screams, blast
fumes, you come with grass-				you
fire, mass corpses, huts					love
blazed; you come with torches				to me.

poor boys   poor boys
who fought the war
fought the war							I love you.

and I marry you
to erase the world.						I love the world.

We beg for sleep
Together we look for

the giver of sleep.

This is love.

If we could pray
we would say this
This is love.

April 1981

STAGGERING OVER THE BRIDGE THAT JOHN BERRYMAN JUMPED FROM

Staring down / into the swirling Black water
Black lines ripple, cross and curve.
The bridge trembles as cars zoom by
behind me. I walk, and
I look over my shoulder
at the lights blinking on Franklin St.
Three Indians lean against the window
of a liquor store and count their pennies.
I approach them. The tall one sticks out his hand.
"Got a quarter, brother?"
"No-no-no," I say, "I gotta match."
The summer is hot. In the Northwoods
thousands of well-fed campers
with portable TVs, CB radios, and butane stoves
flee the raging fires, they flee the raging fires,
and you, old man, who tried to drink the river,
who tried to fight the fire.

born of a woman
(1980)

FROM THE MOMENT

(or, Right / at — The Time)

Right / at / the time she began to count —
To compute, her comings:
"Oh, baby, that / was / five."
The world was void, void, void,
Even her hair caressing my face.

Right / at / the time she spoke so intel / li / gently:
"Marriage is not a union —
It / is / a 50-50 proposition."
The world was void, void, void —
And her / words were / as nothing in empty space.

From the moment she whined,
"You spend your money, and I'll spend mine —
I'll even spend the loot from our mutual crime."—
The world was void, void, void.
From the moment she flew
Into the bloody / blue / arms
Of her pistol / packing brothers,
The world was void, void, void.
The music was void — with holes in the air,
And our laughter was void — falling flat
Against the walls —
And love was void —
And life was void,

And the children of / our / love
Will turn to / pillars / of salt —
If we don't walk the same walk —

And talk the same talk
'Bout being free. and thee. and me.

THREE SONGS

"I was so in love I was miserable"
— Guitar Slim

I. Slim's Song

I knew something was wrong
when he said
I want this whiskey tested
and my money invested
'cause times are bad
just lost the best girl
I ever had.

Of course it didn't last long.
Not after the coconut was opened.
No milk. No milk.
Just bubble, bubble.
Toil and trouble.

We call and call:
it wasn't me.
Me neither —
It wasn't me neither,
neither neighbor.

II. Song of the Reverend Gatemouth Moore

Gatemouth Moore
became a preacher

Now it's The Reverend
Gatemouth Moore.
This is where the wind
begins to stretch

and cling to solids:
like a rock is a rock and
a bird in the sky
is a bird in the sky.

A tornado warning is something else.
Teach them to run
from the enormous funnel.
Sometimes the retarded children
come to play and are ushered
about like lepers.
Teach them to avoid the sickness
that waits in the well.

Bwana this is your game
(bwana mean friend).
Because we have the music —
So, please, come dance —
come dance with me.

      III. Healing Song

The power returns. We remember.
The night of the tennis
The eyes in your garage.
These twins. These twos
glare at you

in and out, up and down.
But it all comes out the same place
and fails to convince.

(Meanwhile in the heart of the city
the night is long and moonless
but the fire is bright
in the hearts of the people.)

It all seems so simple
so I'll tell you where to look
not what to see. "Dr. i-john
the Conqueror" has roots.
He sees. Sometimes the music
makes you want to boogie.

And always the white streets
and ladies departing. Ladies
departing.

Created in fellowship with Robert Slater, K. C., Mo., 1976

FOR DAN BERRIGAN

I don't know about you, whiteman all dressed in black.
I mean I really don't know just where you at.
Maybe you're far ahead of us, or far behind:
Maybe you see it all, whiteman, or maybe you blind.

LOVE SONG TO IDI AMIN

The white / men / are
Boiling poison in
A big / black / pot, are
Shouting out
Omens
By satellites, are / out
To kill you, man,

And the black / men are
Sucking in air — and Idi
Amin — thru rotten teeth, are
Going to fold their arms, are
Going to philosophy, are
Going to / let you die;

But you, love / singer,
Have already won the war;

So when your eyes drink
The swing
of your woman's ass
As she leads you / up / the stairs,
Say: "Sott. Sott.
Sott. Sott. Sott.
Say Sott Sott Sott SottSott
Say SottSottSott."

The white / men are

Out to kill / you / man,
But you — love / singer —
Grinning at women —
Speaking to alligators
By clapping your hands —
Dancing with children
to African bands,
Saying:
"Sott. Sott. SottSott
Sott Sott. SottSottSott."

You, love / singer,
Skinning and grinning
In the African sun —
You / have / already / won
The war.

A POEM FOR 3RD WORLD BROTHERS

So keep your bouncing walk, and
keep your hip and mellow talk. yeah —and
keep your jackknife laughter that shakes the air.
cause white / america would have you move
like cubes. stumbling. without rhythm
or freedom. white / america would design
your dance and your speech by computer —
would have you sit in stiff chairs
and squeeze your knees.
white / america would kill the cat in you.

or they will send their lackeys to kill for them.
and if those negroes fail
white / america will whip out her boss okie doke:
make miss ann lift the hem of her mystic skirt
and flash white thighs in your eyes to blind you
to your own beauty and that of your sisters
who choke back the hurt and hide their love
behind blond wigs and red wine.
and if you ain't dead
by the time white thighs wrap round your head
white / america will send the thrill of the pill
to kill you.
you diggit — you diggit?
to down the red devils is to deal in Blk / death
(makes you fuck over your brothers) cuts you off
from your people, makes you cop out

and roam single — thru this graveyard
of white / america. and your ears will be deaf
to the cries of Blk / children who look to you to
protect them from the white / ghosts.

So keep your bouncing walk. and.
keep your hip and mellow talk. yeah — and
keep your jackknife laughter that shakes the air.
white / america seeks to kill the cat in you
cause white / america knows that fire eyes glow
that Blk / muscles are strong
and that if brothers dance together
freedom won't be long —
you diggit? — you diggit?

WELCOME HOME, ANDREW YOUNG –

I'm / sho / glad that you didn't get Hung:

'Cause no righteous preacher / man
Can sow seeds or sermons that / will / grow
In this season of silliness
Even if you show
Willingness
To high / step to the white / boy's song
There / is / too much wrong
For a right / on Preacher to go along
With the killingest boy
History has / ever / known
Let 'im die, dude, with his lies
Gurgling in his throat —
Come home — do / like / Shine —
Leap off the boat

Under these "Southern Skies"
You / are / the man
To help us deal-for-real
With the Ku Klux Klan

So, Welcome home, Andrew Young —
I'm / sho / glad — you didn't get hung.

COMES NOW THE RED MADNESS

"Nixon really did us a favor, in a way. 'Cause nobody can sit back now, and claim ignorance about the Evil. — Why, man, if him and his buddies hadda got away with it, they would've made Hitler look like a Sunday School teacher."

— Overheard in a pool room

Comes now the red madness.
Words like "law 'n' order" and "peace with honor"
Roll and rattle thru the electric air
And fall / like / snowflakes
On the neat lawns and white picket fences.
Inside our rooms we sweep
The last speck of dirt under the door,
Flick off the lights, creep into our feather beds
And sleep. And our fear, like a lover,
Lies with us. Wide eyes in the darkness.

(Comes now the red madness. The Man.)

A CONVERSATION WITH MYSELF

What am I
        doing here
in these missouri hills
hitch / hiking these hi / ways
              where farmers
fondle their guns
and eye my back
the cars zoom by
              zoom zoom zoom
and disappear around the bend
I sit
on the abutment of a small bridge
and wait
        reading mari evans' book
below me a brook gurgles along
a field of corn, green, waving in the wind
five cows stand swishing their tails
                in the shade
                of three cedars
a hi / way cop passes
             and
             slows down
peering in his rear / view mirror
I clutch
     I am a Black Woman
                  like
a security blanket
I turn and show my teeth

........................and
..................................the book
the cop gasses the engine
..................................and disappears
..................................I scramble
....down
under the bridge
..................and pee in the water
what am I
..........doing here
in these missouri hills
wish
I was / up / in harlem
where
I could talk *bad*.

THE BALLAD OF BETTY DUNN

Betty Dunn was young and black
And Betty was o so pretty —
She dreamed to be a singer
So she "cut out" for the city.
She left her Ma and Pa
To be a singer in the city.

Betty soon met a man
Who played the saxophone.
The music flowing from his horn
Enchanted our Betty Dunn;
The lonesome blues fired the soul
Of tender Betty Dunn.

The music man smiled and winked
As his music found its mark.
Then he took the hand of Betty Dunn
And led her to the dark.
He took her trembling hand
And he led her to the dark.

On the shabby side of town, now
Strolls our Betty Dunn.
The only songs she sings now
Are to her baby son.
She sings her songs now
To her brown-eyed baby son.

CONGRESSMAN HAROLD FORD

He may / be —
"Light, bright —
And damn / near / white"
But he / is / still
Pretty much right.

LOOKING AT THE LAKE WHERE OTIS REDDING LAY

Beneath this body of water
    beneath this shaking swelling belly
    turtle crawl   fish swim   tails flutter
    teeth gnaw the flesh to bare white bone
    the skull rolls under a rock ridge

Beneath this bowl of blue
    Songs rise in the mornings O Otis
    Star of the Southern Bright
    dying cold in this northern lake
    i mourn man for you tonight

LIGHTNIN' HOPKINS ARRIVES IN DETROIT

The lights glare like lanterns of hell
Stars and jets and a half / hidden moon wink and blink
Thru the smog and fog of dee / troit mich / e / khan
Under a bunch of bushes / down / in "The 'Jects"
A 13 / yr / old girl pulls / down / her pants
For a man with one / eye / who cries for his Mother
Meanwhile — out / in / the jungle
A matronly lady with blond hair
Pours poison in her husband's drink
A mother weeps for her son —
Shot in the head in the war in Vietnam
A whore crawls in / to a car and turns a trick
A young poet goes mad — thinking that's what
"Poets" are / spozed / to do
A cops stops a disco dancer and rams his gun
Up her vagina in Lightnin' Hopkins' detroit
General Motors courts the arab oil
And polishes the star of david and
Demands the death of Palestine meanwhile
Back / in / cadillac square the chrysler building
Pierces the air like the impotent erection
That it / is / — meanwhile — as the searchers seek —
And the politicians speak and the priest / class preach —
The music-makers sing — and save —
The citizens of Lightnin' Hopkins' dee / troit.

A SHAKESPEAREAN SONNET: TO A WOMAN LIBERATIONIST

If you knows   where the nose goes
When the doh's close —
Then / why / do   the ho's pose
Wid / doubt no clothes?

— Cause they knows
When the cold / hawk   blows
That / all / two's   and two's
Don't make no fo's.

A PERSONAL LETTER TO ELDRIDGE CLEAVER

Look
      over
            your shoulder,
Brother you are alone (prove
Me wrong).
The folks
        have snuck
Back to their homes
To sit
In their rooms
With their feet
        to
           the
              fire.

Did you forget the joint?
And, how,
    when,
        thingsgottight
All the *bad*
Brothers and grays
Would / talk / about confronting

The warden
        and the guns
In the guard towers?
           and you

Young men with ideals
                        wanting
Freedom for real
            would bleeve the rap
Run way / out front
And chuck the first stone
And
When the heat got hot
Find your
      self in the hole
Alone?
Same shit.
You sit
      there
In your paris cell
While we sit
            here
In our soft chairs
With our feet
To the fire.
(Prove me wrong.)

unpublished poems
(dates unknown)

CURTAINS FOR LINESMEN

The word acts
in its moment, and the audience

is part of the air. I spin
the threads, or wires

of speech. Where I have been
is the more and more tentative

safety of friends,
that two-handed many, that great

stretched web. But where I go
is going to be

silent and high and
stranded.

REJECTIONS

We reject these poems because of the space taken
in sorrow,
that they do not speak of the promised horse of healing.

We reject these bone dark words
because they are joyless in shape
and silent of a rising wind.

Poetry should be easier, forgiven like,
not drug from innards,
too much of old men in dying light,
those moon sorrowed people
living in sexless rooms.

Put this darkness back into your pen.
Don't mail this scorpion again.

Submit something of a turn lifting,
the beginning of the sun about all frozen,
written fully in a day of light.

LOSERS

When today begins and yesterday ends
and darkness unfolds into light;
And our future of dreams is not as it seems
and reality is within sight;
The first thing we say as our souls fade away,
"Who's to say what's wrong or right?"
Then we make alibis while our friends criticize
leaving no one to help with the fight!

WINNERS

I'm a black man in a hell of a land
its structure once sturdy is shaking;
As my people decide to play past genocide
revolution is now in the making!
We'll end our frustration with self-education
in pursuit of, our lives we are staking;
Since the pig won't get hip and come off his trip,
we believe our freedom is worth taking!!!

UNSEEN DEFINITION

It is not right for those to speak to me
To speak of freedom
Who have the wrong definition of freedom
It is not right for those to speak to me
To speak of love
If they have never felt the meaning of love

Love and freedom
What words they are
Yet look at the fruits of the action thereof
Is this life all that life should be?
Consider...
Freedom itself can be an empty shell
Without a greater cause
For just as an empty shell is free
Without inner substance
So can one be
If freedom is another word
For an unseen definition
Of a principle in secret code.

FUCK NOW / PAY LATER

Sister I'm sorry you see lust in my eyes;
The lust for your body I've grown to despise;
A lust which forces my nature to rise,
And neglect revolution to get to your thighs.
I know this is not where my true freedom lies,
And I know for our cause it is truly unwise;
But it's hard to control when you show me your thighs,
And auction your body in Western disguise.
Sister I'm sorry you see lust in my eyes;
But you help put it there with those beautiful thighs;
In a sex sick society we just don't realize,
That we're programmed to fuck but not to survive!

AT DELOS

I have come to protest,
above the empty treasury shaft,
the deep quarry where they came,
and I stand before the archaic holy
lions with their round jaws
and take the sign out of my pocket,
unfold it, hold it up
and let them see it, let them
read my placard. Now I am moving
down the line of old emperors,
bearded, whipped by rain,
half-fallen into the sea,
here where even the winds turned round.

PRELUDE TO A SEPTEMBER STORM

Black clouds bounce about like angry cattle
With lightning leaping from their stomping hooves;
The thunder gods make ready for battle,
And the wind is a giant that frets and moves

With flat feet through this crackling September.
Mama grabs sheets from the fence and keeps one eye
On her baby — who is the sole member
Of the house that casts no frown at the sky.

PIN PRICKS OF LONELINESS

When I become lonely I
Think of a tree in winter, alone,
Casting its slim shadow down a snowy slope,
But that does me no good.
I think of summer and an old man
Dozing in the park, cane between his legs.
But that does me no good.
I think of spring and a woman washing her hair —
Long lovely locks of sheeny black.
With the suds and sun's glare making
Diamonds bubble in the morning air.
But that does me no good.
I think of fall and my favorite nights:
Saturday. Beer in the taverns and girls
Snapping their fingers to the blues.
But that does me no good.
When I am loneliest, I
Pick up my pen and cry
Blue lines of tears
And that appears
To do me good.

STILL GOING STRONG BLUES

Well, I never thought you'd leave me, baby,
Even tho I know I've done you wrong;
One side of my bed is empty
And all your clothes are gone;
Yeah, and tho I've cried a tub of tears,
I am still going strong.

Sometimes I weep and moan, Lady,
Sometimes I stay out all night long
Shooting craps and smoking dope —
Doing ev'rything I *know* is wrong,
But when I wake / up in the morning
I'll still be going strong.

Lord, they locked / me in their jail, baby,
And then they threw away the key;
The fbi sicced bloodhounds on my trail, baby,
And the judge ignored my plea;
But even if they tap my phone —
And even if I get cancer at the bone,
You can / bet your bottom dollar
That I'll keep / on keeping on.

Well they say don't have no babies
And they say don't have no friends —
They make men look like women —
They make women look like men.

Said they locked / me up in their jails, mama,
They even tried to hush my song;
The white / boys laughed at me, mama,
And some brothers laughed right / along;
But when the sun rises and the laughter's gone —
Don't you know I'll still be going strong.

THE BLUE DUCK

An idea can be glazed, captured, brought down
From heaven!
Our feathers can become blue,
Even a beak can smile!
This duck crouches in a world that cannot
Break it, says Open our eyes,
Let them become luminous,
Amused, and kind!
Duck says to so much: I am not interested.
Duck says Let us feel this blue floating
Down from heaven, let us have thoughts
Between us, let us be fearless.
Duck says Consider the dumbness of animals,
How wonderful it is not to care about death,
To go on falling away from this worst nature
That has been patted upon us like clay.
Duck says we can sit still and go on swimming
Toward the infinite.
Duck says we do not have to judge
With pleasure or displeasure or tell
Ourselves it is all for the best or not.
Duck shows us how naked he is,
How obscene it is to wear a helmet.
Duck says, even to Sunday crowds,
We are lovers, we are without purpose!

BRING IT HOME BLUES

When you left me, baby
I stayed / up / all night long —
I watched the door — I paced the floor —
I listened for the telephone.

So bring / it / on home
      (bring it on home)
Bring / it / on HOME — bring / it / on home.
Let me tell you, Lady
What it's all about —
I need your kind / of / love.
It makes me wanna jump and shout.
So bring / it / on home
      (bring it on home)
Bring / it / on HOME — bring / it / on home.

Oh my lovely lady
Listen to my song.
You don't have to worry
I / ain't / gon do / you / no wrong —
So bring / it / on home
      (bring it on home)
Bring / it / on HOME — bring / it / on home.

PARTS

the night had just
                begun
                        Indianapolis far behind
nothing in the future but the night
      & a big neon sign
bordering the
      flesh

all
   the
 eyes
have it
   it continues to rain
& the colors in the
night
   begin to fade
her face
 still
   guides my feet

the imagination again
"stirring dull roots"
the actual woman there
but the image was remote
from the actuality, & tho
I'd like to remake it,
shoot this grand meeting again
with all the dream accoutrements,

it's still only
the semblance of what it
should be

Indulgently, I remember
her breasts in the shower at the Holiday Inn,
alert to the feel of the jet of warm water
& earlier the clean sheets
against our tired bodies
too anxious
       to sleep

a mass of subtle freckles on her
       upper back above the bra strap

the drab Chicago street far below
       I stretched to touch it unsure of where
             I was
& fell thru

reminded as I fell
of the variety of things
to touch

END OF AN ARM

(For Orleans)

long fingers
of inlets
& coves
fist of
sparkles
i
remember
the miles
of soft curves
her feet moved
the cold wet
the black
sparkles all
i could see
in the black
she
was far away the
tide came in & she
was no longer
the wet
& the sparkles
the soft curves
to caress
with toes & dream
the long fingers
of coves
& inlets open
on

my days & nights
she
is in a fist of
sparkles
sand in the
sheets
again
sheets
of dark
sheets
of sparkles
in the cool
night
of the
shore
i remember
so clearly
as if
bathed in light
& night
now pressing
those soft & gentle fingers
closing
gesture now
opening

LOSSES

here was a woman who I felt a need to kiss
& I did kiss her lower back, her face & lips
held her hands as often as allowable
that that was enough. she didn't say much, so
there wasn't much to be said. she didn't hold me
much & I didn't mind that so much that I knew it.
that it meant so much to touch her & hold her &
kiss her that one-way streets didn't matter
that she might say goodbye forever to me tomorrow
& that wouldn't matter. that that touch could
be so important. so climactic. yet still only go so far
that I didn't plumb the depth of how important that was,
that intrinsic feel for her. that it could be gone so soon,
unrecoverable. & that that wouldn't matter so much that
I would regret, that no pain would come that didn't
pass in the morning. yet the sense that there was
something so important here. that suns & moons would
pale. that everything else would likely have subsided
had it grown. that I am completely alone again, that I
was completely alone then but wouldn't allow that as
a fact then. that its only seeming importance is that
in its being gone I feel I touched paradise one day
in a dream

NO, I CAN'T GO TO JAMAICA THIS YEAR... I'M GOIN TO JAIL INSTEAD

(Dedicated to the "Beale Street Six"
and all people in jails everywhere)

My friend Vivian lusts after Jamaica
She's been there three times now
She tries to lure me there each year,
with stories of white beaches and tropical sunsets and good times
But I can't go this year...
I'm goin to jail instead

Now, I like white beaches and tropical sunsets,
And I like brown-skinned folks and good times,
And I like the round rhythms of reggae music,
And mangoes
And each year I say I'll go,
But I can't go this year...
I'm goin to jail instead

Gonna get me a glimpse of Justice in action
Gonna get me a taste of jailbird stew
Gonna test the new bunks and the stainless-steel toilets
with water fountains riding piggy-back
Gonna take a crash course in penology

Sure, I'd like to go and frolic in a tropical paradise
But there's work to / be / done
Freedom Songs to / be / sung
And Struggles to / be / won
No, I can't go to Jamaica this year...
I'm goin to jail instead

I TRY TO TOUCH YOUR GRIEF

You are quiet,
a white sea bird
blinding me
with wide wet wings,
stuffing my mouth
with feathers.

You fly, dip,
beak shining
into silent water
and rise
unburdened
by fat slippery fish.

From the shore where I stood
I row out towards you.
I spit out the feathers that choked me
and call you.

My voice leaves a wake across the water
and breaks the grace
of your flight.

JAZZ HAIKU #2

The knobby black fingers plucked
Golden notes
From the slender guitar.

JAZZ HAIKU #3

Sing, tall woman, sheathed in satin;
The white eyes watch with
Open mouths

SONS OF THUNDER

The sun rose red behind green hills
About the sea of Galilee
When Jesus came for John and James,
The fisher of Zebedee.

Come two bold boys without a word:
James, quick and strong; John, tall and thin.
They dropped their nets to follow Christ,
To fish for the souls of men.

Zebedee raved and stomped the deck,
His booming voice set sails asunder.
And Jesus smiled and called the boys —
Boanerges — The Sons of Thunder.

KATIE LADY – WON'T YOU PLEASE COME HOME

(Or, — Pick / up / the Skillet, Millet)

Who roam so / far / from the Fury
From the center
        of the Storm
        in your coming
        and your going
We need you here   shed a tear
For Jo Ann Little
And Karen Ann Quinlin
        who have / no / hope
Of hacking the rope
That breaks their necks
        Free the women
Of the Cherokee Nation
        Free the women
Of the Tribes of Abraham
        Free the women
From the War Maker
        Free the women
Of the Ku Klux Klan
        Free the women
Here — In this graveyard of greenbacks.
We stray so / far / from the source of the sin
Where Eve continues to take "the blame" for men.

A POEM FOR OUR PRESIDENT: WHOSE NAME, RONALD REAGAN, BEARS THE NUMBER OF THE BEAST

I hear a child say,
"He's a mean old man!"
I hear the young men say,
"I will not die, I will not lie
In the mud for old men
Who dream of death and blood."
I hear the young women say,
"I will not follow a father
Who rapes his daughter
And beats my mother."
I hear a nodding junkie say,
"Man, Nancy needs to give the dude some pussy!"

SHARECROPPING ECONOMICS 101

Our Father who / up / in Heaven:
White man owed me 'leven, but pay / me / seven.

Thy Kingdom come, Thy Will be done:
But if I hadn't took that, I wouldn't got none!

LIFE?

In the beginning we were one,
Living to add light to the sun,
Living to speed but not to run,
Living in peace without a gun.

In the end we are none,
Dying of love turned into fun,
Dying to see no change begun,
Dying with much work left undone.

SONG TO THE GREAT MOTHER

She is a mountain, is my mother,
This woooman who rides the River,
Who rides this flow
Before me.

The Sun on your cheeks,
Like "Pillars of Gold,"
Lighting you, lighting you.

"I am a woooman / and my song
Is circular,
I am a woooman / and my song
Is circular.

INTRODUCTION

Some can win and some can lose,
life they call this game,
in spite of if we win or lose,
we end up all the same.

In this game I play a pawn.
The queen can move at will,
she puts my body in her mind
to see what makes me real.

With concepts towards a free world,
my insight hurts her pride.
The king, her jealous ally,
resorts to genocide.

TURNPIKE LANDSCAPE

Scalped is truly the word
for this much improved land,
worked upon with pioneer
hardware
so that the trucks roll now
over what is a barrenness
except for the cattle
which must be raised up in life
because death is not yet perfect
and complete,
though in this whiteness
it is almost.

WHAT WE MAKE OF IT

This is the life: six deep
in a bed, twelve feet
of friends and a foot
of comforter. Outside,
where we keep
predictabilities
of tree and hill, a weather
improvises: leaves, this time,
a trash of dollar bills,
a hurricane of squirrels, an edge
of threat.
But this is the alternative:
a stove in the living room
to hoard its nest of coals
for our excitement.
In a word, a warmth.
In a sense, a measure

of music or time or believe or whatever
it is we separately make.

This is the pleasure.

THE SCHOLAR ENVIOUS OF HIS NEIGHBOR

I turn the page.
Next door he moves from one breast to the other.

FOUR VIEWS

      I.

My two eyes look the same
But one sees
Skeletons, bleached in the sun

      II.

Two worlds come together
At the point of eye and ear.

      III.

A man walking the rocky shore
Of New England
Doesn't know I'm
On the other side of the ocean

      IV.

On rainy days
The sun is remembered
In the shape of
A diamond on a rich woman's hand

NEW YORK CITY

New York City
Yeah, New York City
Big fat funky New York City
And all the people are poor in New York City
Poor in body, poor in soul, poor in spirit in New York City
New York City
Yeah, New York City
Is fat and bloated like a dying old lady.
The steel, the straining steel —
The people squirm like worms in New York City.
You got to be hip in New York City — I mean —
You got to be hippy dippy. You got to make it, baby
"Do yo thing" got to get over "push your program"
Got to get over
In New York City

THE READING TOUR

N. lit up a joint on Wabash St. in Chicago
between Greyhounds on the way to read at the
Hummingbird Cafe in Indianapolis —
anxiety is his companion on the road
a rained out reading in Ithaca to a reading in
Baltimore where nobody came & they drank wine
instead to New York City where he couldn't find
a reading
anxiety
strange cities, strange people, audiences, no
audience
no place to go home to at night
instead the busses move on night & day — dreary terminals
& junk food
he eats so much to feed his nerves
he gains 20 pounds
so that he fits my pants which he has to borrow
food — to ease him. & reefer risked on a city street
&
when he got here — friends, reception he could feel
under his scarred skin,
relations to carry back on the good ship Greyhound
gleaming silver in the Iowa sun.

I REMEMBER MINNIE

I remember Minnie the Moocher,
Subject of speculation and joke of drunks,
Pathetic pusher of a rusty cart,
Hoarder of trinkets, keeper of trunks
Holding treasures only for boys and puppies,
Timeless mother of the world
Whose heart no one knew
Nor took the time to know.

PRAYERS OF A PRISONER

In my youth I bowed before
The gods of gold;
And my soul knew no peace
Because greed had shut the door
To love, and my heart was cold.
I fell from Thy grace
Into this place of wet stone.
My days are shadows, faceless
And gray. I am alone.
Without Thee there is no light
To guide me from this darkness
Into the bright
Glow of Thy Glory.

O God! grant me relief;
Grant me patience in my grief;
Have mercy, O Lord, on me, a thief.

WAITING FOR TRIAL AFTER WATTS

Well... yes; the heat last summer *was* something else —
that's true; and, sure, my woman was fretting; and, sure,
I needed dough for a "do." — But you speak of sparks and
    socio-economical factors.
Well, the fact is, my mellow man, it was a song, a belly song.
The singing began before I was born, before Bird or Du Bois or
    Father Divine
before the sun, stars, and moon. It was the eternal concert of
    sound and motion and counterpointing.
The flaming, falling joints were soon beats beats. Glass crashed
    at Sharps.
Rifles cracked in the streets. Slim shadows trembled against
    walls and
telephone posts. I danced the Frug with Vachel Lindsay while
Leopold's ghosts shrieked fear in Whitey's face.
Deconstruction, you say? But, baby, a man must move — he must
    create
or destroy. God wills it. Mob madness, you say? I wasn't mad —
    I was sad.
And even now I have no joy. Yeah, baby — later.

Your honor! Your Honoreski! If it be
your pleasure, I make a motion to suppress, to oppress,
to quash the evidence less I plead patience and progress
and illegal search and seizure.

PERSONAL PROPERTY

I own not the car I possess
or the home in which I live
I own not my fancy clothes
or the charity that I give
but what I own is priceless
precious as mundane gold
all that I shall ever own
is the life within my soul

[COMING TO YOU]

Coming to you
I took a chance
and in my way
I'm glad of it.

Softly I leave
wondering why
we did and again
why we shouldn't.

My thoughts come fluently.
Why do words stumble
Like a crippled wild thing?

I must suffer my own
non-being.
My self-denial must
be borne by me.

POLITICS

The dog pauses before the fire,
watches, gains
weight, can't make
light of it, lies
heavy down. Geese
freeze to the lake. The snake
wears a bad new wrinkle,
bark. The trees
lie, rustling skins
and squirrels
fib, the purses
of their faces full. The bear
begins to snore and every
outdoor animal expires
a rich white lie of air.
Even you are taken in.
It is not winter.

MALCOLM

Malcolm X said, "The white man
is a devil."
I try to get my friends to take this seriously
but they are all white men.

GENOCIDE

Genocide genocide
That's the reason Malcolm died
That's the reason Nixon lied
That's the reason mothers cried
Genocide genocide
That's why on old Miles they lied
Said his music's style had died
They wouldn't know they've never cried
Genocide genocide
That's the reason Martin died
The CIA has always spied
The FBI has never tried
Genocide genocide
That's the reason Hendrix died
He changed hard rock into black pride
And all the freaks were on his side
Genocide genocide
That's why black universities died
Their true black founders long denied
It's said the students never tried
Genocide genocide
The year when Shirley Chisholm tried
The year Amerikan money died
The red Chinese can't be denied
Genocide genocide
It's hard for us to coincide
Black and white cannot decide
White minds dwell on phony pride

Genocide genocide
Do you know why George Jackson died?
Why Angela's case has so long been tried?
Why H. Rap Brown was forced to hide?

    Genocide!

IOWA DEAD

By the river town
the little old ladies go
down with flowers for the dead
of eight wars, only sixteen
sides that fought
with justice

THE SURVIVORS

We remember now
Grandmothers who had
Children by the litter.

Letters are sent
As far away as
Oregon in search

Of a father.
The survivors are
All but forgotten:

The anonymous ones
The ones we inspired
The ones we pestered.

The sides are chosen.
The forces aligned.
Our work is done.

We who in the beginning
Were such an influence
Are left to mind the fences.

TERMS

Ten below, and my ancestors
grow tight-lipped in the grave,
but keep their grip (stand
their ground), their rocks
half frozen off, their eyes
as chipped and false as pyrite.
Underneath the snow's two tons
of sun, they bear me
malice, brandishing old trees.

I turn my back:
an unscarred
meadow opens up, a stranger's
generosity, a brightness
empty of regard, till I can see
as far as blind diviners do: past
January, past the accident
of kindnesses, past plan.
I'm my family's last.

MARCH IN A BEANFIELD

Last harvest's beans
hover stiff over
the new green
and brother I surrender
with nothing to keep
me from sinking.
The weathered stalks
weave in
and out of the ground.
Emptiness everywhere but
here green closes the sky
and the blackbird's call
is almost remembered
in my body.
This is where I lose
myself to the terrible
rushing inside me.
From so far away
you hold me here
and I tremble against
the newness of flesh.

uncollected poems

THE POINT OF THE WESTERN PEN

(for my son, Etheridge Bombata)

Where come we from? and so forth?
The point of the western pen is red
With the blood of us. The pages of Harlem,
Timbuctoo, Waycross, flutter
And float on the midnight waters
And turn to flowers.

Where come we from? and so forth?
The point of the western pen is red
With the blood of us. You, me.
The sages sing.
We sunflowers facing the east,
Dancing in the wind and folding at night.

Under the noon-day light
We drop, red petal by red petal
Into the mid-night waters,
Into the rushing, swirling waters.
Where come we from? and so forth?
The point of the western pen is red
With the blood of us.

THINGS AWFULLY QUIET IN AMERICA

(Song of the Mwalimu Nkosi Ajanaku)

Things awfully quiet in America, yeah —
Much too quiet in America.
We / been abused, confused, and misused too long —
We / done played too long — done prayed too long —
Say things too quiet in America.
We're wearing three-piece suits, and cowboy boots;
We're wearing animal skins, and dry-dry grins —
Sing things too quiet in America
In America "Revolution" is never heard;
Our historical shit is never stirred;
In America "Revolution" is a dirty word,
So things stay quiet in America.
Ghetto rats still bite in America;
Empty bellies ache at night in America,
And Seniors shake with fright in America.
There's a war going on in America,
And we're killing our sons in America,
In the many, many prisons in America.
Things awfully quiet in America, yeah —
Much too quiet in America.
Need to "Raise a Ruckus Tonight" in America;
Need to fight-the-fright in America,
Make the fire-eyes bright in America,
Cause things ain't right in America
Black folks're sad, and mad, in America,
And that's too bad in America.
They say: "Things ain't changed in America;

'The Man' is still deranged in America."
They say: "What went wrong in America? —
Where's the 'Freedom Song' in America?"
We / gonna set things right in America,
Cause things too quiet in America, yeah —
Much too quiet in America.

ON THE REMOVAL OF THE FASCIST AMERICAN RIGHT FROM POWER

Come on, you too, whoo / doo, we can do it,
You can do it, truck driver, you can,
Cab driver, you can do it, take away
Their power! you can do it,
High school student, you can, you can do it,
College student, take it, take it away,
They have no right to it anymore,
They have *betrayed* the American Revolution!
It's yours, take it back, Grandmother.
FREEDOM FOR ALL AMERICANS FIRST!
You can do it, Stop them from selling Death,
Speak, you / gay / man with streaks in your hair,
You can do it, Gay woman with sad eyes,
You can do it, Black man, take it,
In the Name of Crispus Attucks, take it,
In the Name of Frederick Douglass, take it!
FUCK THE FOREIGN THOUGHT! take it,
Take back the American Revolution
From the big daddies and the little wives,
You can do it, White man, take it,
In the Names of Lincoln, Paine, Adams,
Jefferson, you know who, White man,
Take back the Revolution from the Fascists
In the Names of John Brown and Martin King,
Take it, you can do it, take it from them:
The American Ayatollahs: Jerry Falwell,
Billy Graham, Oral Roberts, Kahane,
And the Mormon maniacs, wrap yourselves

In Betsy Ross's Flag, it was meant for
You, white man, so take it back, say NO
To your Fathers, Say NOOOOO!
Say FREEDOM! SAY FREEEEDOOOOM!
Say FREEDOM FOR ALL AMERICANS FIRST!
Say FUCK THE FOREIGN THOUGHT!
FROM THE EAST OR THE WEST, OR BOTH!
You can do it, farmer man, you can,
You can do it, Latino, Native man, you can,
GrandFather, take it, tell them:
FREEDOM FOR ALL AMERICANS FIRST
Is in "our national interest,"
Come on, you intellectual left, you can do it,
Teach us Jeffersonian Principles, teach us,
Teach us the thoughts of Adams, Du Bois, and Black Elk —
FUCK THE FOREIGN THOUGHT! you can do it,
O Black woman, O white woman, O Mothers,
You can do it, take it take away their power,
In the Names of Susan Anthony, Harriet Tubman,
In the Names of Emma Goldman, Sojourner Truth,
In the Name of Betsy Ross, Take back the D.A.R.,
Overrun the League of Women's Voters, you can do it,
Be the true Daughters of the American Revolution!
Encircle the lil wives of the Big Daddies in a Dance,
A Revolutionary Dance, confront the lil wives
With Revolutionary Songs, you can do it, you can,
Say NO, say NOOOOO!
You can take their power away, you can,
You can do it, with the Good Power, the Right
Power that comes from the Left, the heart / side,
you can do it,
Say FUCK THE FOREIGN THOUGHT!
Say FREEDOM FOR ALL AMERICANS FIRST!
Say FREEDOM! say FREEEDOOOM!

THE NIXON FLU

(For Drs, Scott and Benecek)

What the WORD will do!
When the Doctor's song
Is 'bout the Hong
              Kong flu
When it is we
     Who are killing
And coughing
With the Nixon Flu
And his mama and pat and tricia too....
(that's called a nigga playing the dozens)

WHO KNOWS ???

Like Pinnochio's...?
When the doors /
                close
On the Oval office,
Maybe Reagan's nose
Grows... red (like Rage
And Sin and Blood),... ignores
The good and sage /
                advice
Of his psychic /
                soul:
White / lies are not nice;
Like it,
      or not, they won't suffice
For the truth, the truth,
Black and black, and holy /
                whole;
Contrary to the imaginary
                Pinnochio's nose —
Fiction ain't fact.
Contrary to the Contras,
Contrary to the Contra /
                vening
Of advisory Moles,
Beribboned and bereft,
Contrary to the keening
Of Iran and Iraq —
Right may be Left,

But white ain't black
And a lie ain't the truth!
So. So. So suppose...
The cancerous growth
On the imperial, and presidential,
      nose
Is the surreal, and the essential
      proof —
Like Pinnochio's
Who knows? — who knows???

MEMO #75

Iran and Iraq
Attack and attack!
"Still Waters" now rough
In the Persian Gulf —
Those mines do not bluff.

HIP / NOTES TO MY / SELF

(or, six haiku)

The lake listens... trees
Tremble... black crows caw?
"We / gonna / bomb Nicaragua!"

Lila! — lips like lilacs!
Memphis moon... your perfume...
O me! — miles from Mississippi!

Detroit's summer sun's
Outrage: three black boys hunting
Coke-cans finds a corpse.

Snow blows... the squirrels pose...
This New Year is two days old —
And I'm two hundred.

Philadelphia!
"City of brotherly love"
(If you're white'n' not MOVE.)

Lunch with her laid me.
Wong's food was fine. But the feast
Was forming in her eyes.

I AM A TREE, MY LOVERS FLY TO AND FROM ME

1.

She appeared, soaring out the sunset
of San Francisco, leaving Hayakawa and his cops.
She brought smiles and flutters, black babies
and a white dog who would eat no bones.
I was a boy then, non-born and bred among
bricks and bars. I was a boy then, and I trembled
before her beauty, and her might. I felt fright,
and I bent and shook and leaned and would not
stand still. And she flew away. Zoom.

2.

She came, zooming outta New York with the sun
in her hair. Her smiles were white teeth. Her breasts
were plums in my mouth. We rode south thru the night.
Her thighs were warm and soft like summer,
And our love was thick and spilled like milk
under the Missouri sky. There was water and laughter
and friends bringing gifts. I was a man then, but
still afraid, and stones began to grow in our bed.

DEARLY / — BELOVED / — MIZZEE

(For Elizabeth Gordon McKim)

Dearly — Beloved — Mizee —
I know that / this surprises Thee —
That / this honey-loving Bear
Rumbled outta his lair
Here
In ye olde Framingham
To detective you unaware,
With your white / ass / bare
Cavorting with an / other / Sam —
Bo Diddly, do-wop-de-wop-wop.

O I / do love / Thee; and if you should / ever / stop
Loving me — my blood would jam
In my veins; my breath would take
Leave of my lungs, rattling, flop-flop-
Ping, like a slave in chains;
My knees would tremble, my hands would shake
Like a Memphis crap-shooter wooing Chance;
My heart would quiver, and break,
Like a Florida oak in a hurricane.

So, I'm glad (and oh so sad) that you're gone
Away from your free and easy home.
So I'm walking this dark and green path alone —
Making this sad, and silly, poem —
Singing our blue, and true, romance.

[IT IS A BITCH NO BREAK]

It is a bitch no break
A purple mysterious bitch
To make a poem in this Library
The ghosts of poets escape book covers
And hover over my shoulder
And snitch to their god of the dead
Their words are not much read here
Their memories rust in the mold.
I am alone and cold.
Besides, I am covered with the cloak of Jah
All the gods I follow are women
And they are all living gods
When I seek just one
I look into the eyes of my mother
Or the eyes of my lover

HAIKU FOR THE HOMELESS

O sister of mine!
I see you in the flat shadows:
An angel fallen.

X-mas crowd patters past,
Red and green lights blink and blink.
Happy Hanukkahs

Match Christian cheers.
Winter's wind tears her beggar's bag,
Alone in the drone

My sister's sorrow
Groans: Shame! Shame! Shame! My sister's
Eyes moan: Blame! Blame! Blame!

A POEM FOR LINCOLN UNIVERSITY

Lincoln is pretty, like a woman in Springtime
the grass is green and the birds sing.
But.
The Brothers
           who say they are Men
are ripping off the sisters /
And the Sisters who say
                   We are Women
are allowing the brothers to rip them off.

And the white students, most of them,
come just to get good grades (and they do)
so they can make a lot of money......
They have no love for Lincoln.

The Black Brothers from the Civil War
are turning over in their graves...............

FOR HUEY P. NEWTON
A BLK / LEADER

(Who ain't got no Hole in his Soul)

Welcome back, brother, from the House of Many Slams
Welcome back to this bigger Babylonian Slams
Welcome back! — And I feel good! — Like
A Blk / Poet sung to me when I hit the bricks:
Huey's back! "I feel like drinking wine
In the alleys and dancing in the streets."

Welcome. We have — in these midnight months —
Missed your keen courage and blazing mind
And we have *needed* your love — that wide Blk / Love
That I can see in your eyes
      When you smile at Blk / Children
That I can hear in your voice
      When you talk to The People
That I can feel in your heart
      When you move toward The Enemy

Right on, brother, right on to Freedom — and the mothers
Of Blk / America will sing to their children
Of Huey Newton, mighty warrior / leader who didn't
Let no devil woman put no hole in his soul
And no devil dude put no shank in his back.

Welcome, Huey, to these *mean* bricks —
I feel like drinking wine in the alleys
And dancing in the streets.

SONG OF THE HOMELESS

I am not Br'er Boll Weevil
Looking for fresh cotton;
I am not the red umbrella
On the subway seat, forgotten
By a lady in a fashionable suit
I am not a Wall Street broker
Selling junk bonds, nor a junkie
Selling toothpaste on 42nd St.
I am a Homeless Person in this
Land of the Free, a Homeless slave
In this Land of the Brave

JUNKY'S SONG

THE PAIN, SO REAL, so intense,
Like a sliver of steel through the eyeball
Into the brain, rocks my mind, rocks my soul,
Feels like a million different pieces.
I am not one, I am not whole;
A war, me against my / self / (and THEM against me too,)
Rages in my head.
My stomach so violently quakes,
Every tormented inch of me cries, screams,
Every tormented inch of me shakes.
The Walls, not bobby frost's, but the warden's,
Coming, tumbling, crushing down / on / me.
Hands reaching out, coming oh so close…
A devil dances in my face, an angel too,
Moving all / about / whispering *overdose*….
"The cessation of pain and sorrow,
And the LOVE and *Joy* of tomorrow,
Is so close, is oh so close…."
But.
I didn't have any "stuff" — "It ain't true."
Said I did what I do, when I / am / sober, and to my / self / true….
The devious devil and innocent angel / are / in my brain;
They are slick, they know every trick,
Living in my head and heart, trying to drive me insane.

Father Time, then blackest of blackness, standing still.

LEAVING INDIANA
AFTER X-MAS, 1987

I hitch a ride to the Air / Port
With a dude named "Red"
Who works as a Sky / Cap
In the Air / Port, who is a man,
And a proper / person. Red said:

"In my book, money talks, (including tips),
And bullshit walks, and bullshit
Is alright, in fact with bullshit I find no fault—
It's just that money talks, in *my* book."

I never see my children, I complain,
And count the coins in my jeans.
My mother is old and arthritic, I complain,
And I count the few coins in my jeans.
Fortune does not favor me, I sing
Is fewness forever my fare.

HAT QUESTIONNAIRE

1. The hat of the future — what it will be like.

In the future, hats and caps will have *more* soft crowns and bills, not the hard crowns and visors which are popular when a people are warmongers and imperialists.

2. List the most famous hats in history.

The Iron Mask, Prez's pork-pie, the English Derby of Dr. Watson, Bella Abzug hats, Che Guevara Beret, Monk's hats.

3. How do you shop for a hat?

Since I have a big head (7 5/8) my first consideration is size — then softness. I spend very little time shopping for a hat — since I already have an idea of what I want.

4. Name "the most virtuous hat." You may want to relate several anecdotes about it.

The most virtuous hat to me is the wide-brimmed, straw hat worn by po' farmers in the south. Tho you didn't ask, the most infamous hat is the military "garrison" hat and helmet.

5. Describe your most beloved headgear.

My most beloved headgear *now* is the beret of the African Freedom Fighter and the "bonnet" of po' southern women.

6. Why wear a hat at all?

For protection and status.

[This piece appeared in "The Hat Issue" of *Milk Quarterly* (1978) in which the editor, Peter Kostakis, featured "completed questionnaires" by writers, artists, and musicians including Joe Brainard, Marion Brown, Leroy Jenkins, Erica Jong, Alex Katz, John Lennon, Claes Oldenburg, Yoko Ono, James Schuyler, Joffre Stewart, and Anne Waldman.]

WARNING

This / is / the Lair
Of "de smoking Bear"
Enter Ye / all who dare
To breathe this polluted air
(— But, for truth, and for Fair,
It ain't no / worse in here
Then it is out there.)

[Posted on the door of Etheridge Knight's Writing Room, 108 Winthrop Rd., Brookline, MA]

THREE HAIKU

O praying mantis
Facing me, Kneeling, Why?
I hold no dominion

I watch from afar
The fisher folk on Fall Creek.
It's spring, and I'm sick.

The car accident
Broke my bones. On the ward
I drove my ghost away.

BLUES FOR A LADY IN BOSTON

I went to sleep last night with your voice ringing in my ears,
Fell asleep last night, o your voice ringing in my ears —
well, you sounded so lonely and o so full of fears.

I woke up this morning just about the break of day.
O the day was dawning when the Furies started to play.
Thinking about you in Boston — o so faraway.

O I get this jones every time you brush your hair,
Said I get this jones every time you brush your long brown hair,
I know this love of mine will follow you everywhere.

So let's boogie in Boston, let's scream and shout, let's do —
Let's dance and sing and make our dreams come true.
           (softly)

About you and me, and Freedom too —
'Bout you and me, and Freedom too.

unpublished poems
(1982-1991)

FREEDOM CHANT FOR BLUE MT. CENTER

Women sang "stone"
Men sang "wood"

Spirit in de wood / stone O I call to Thee
Spirit in de wood / stone O I call to Thee:
Come to BlueMountain — and make me Free...
AAIIEE SIMILO! AAIIEE SIMILO!

Spirit in de wood / stone, O I call Thy Name
Spirit in de wood / stone, drive away my pain
O keep the Center safe til I return again
AAIIEE SIMILO! AAIIEE SIMILO!

When de Spirit come upon the Scene,
She / He drps de petals from dah tree,
She / He shove BlueMountain into dah sky
She / He shove dah river into the sea...

O Spirit in de wood / stone, make de fear go way....
O Spirit in de wood / stone, make me FREE today....
O keep this Center safe, and free, I pray.
AAIIEE SIMILO! AAIIEE SIMILO!

(Repeat as many times as the Spirit moves You.)

YOUR SONG AIN'T REALLY BLUE

(For William "Sonny" Ford)

There / is / a Song inside of you
That / is / as / bright as the Eastern moon;
So when Demons dance inside of you,
When you feel your Song is a sad, sad tune,
Remember the joy in your Belly glows
And the Belly knows:
Your Song ain't really blue —
Your Song ain't really blue.

SOME DAYS

Some days slip by
      like clouds in the sky,
Or the glimpse of a girl
From the edge of the eye.

CONTINUATION BLUES

Well I / woke / up this morning —
Lord, and I don't know south from north,
Lying here looking / out / my window, Lord —
And I don't know south from north —
Just watching the Fall wind blowing
The dead leaves back and forth.

There's a little red red robin
Singing in a cedar tree —
There's a brave lil robin
Singing just as pretty as can be.
Lord — that damn / fool / robin's
Gotta be as confused as me.

BETTY BLUES

I say when my Betty left me
When she walked out the door
I say, she looked over her shoulder
Said, Man — I don't love you any more

And I cried, Lord Lord Lord
What's po' me gonna do —
I feel like water aint wet
I feel like the sky sho / aint blue

My baby shook one hip — And
Then she shook the / other
She said, I'm leaving lil boy
She said, I'm sending you back / to mother

And I cried, Lord, Lord, Lord
What's po' me gonna do
Cause I love that hip-shaking Betty
Like a clover bee loves the dew

FOR HONEY

Unlike your Father and your Mother
Your other sister and brother
Neither in Yahweh, Allah, Buddha
Over any of the other Patriarchs do I believe,
And yet I grieve — I grieve
For you, as if I were a Jew
At the Wailing Wall, or if I were a monk
In a yellow robe, running in flames
Thru the streets of Saigon, I grieve
Emmett Till's Mama moaning in the hot
Mississippi afternoon.

THE FIREMAN SPEAKS OF SMOKE DETECTORS

(For the 7 dead in a 2 room N. Philly Apt.)

The TV lights glare. The White Light
Of Authority graces the Great liar.
The chief speaks of overheated wires
Borrowed by neighbors
Not of overcrowded lives
Robbed by neglect, "Unpaid utility bills,"
Not of unemployment.

The Chief speaks
Of the need for "smoke detectors"
Not the need for New Housing.

The Chief grief is as Formal as his uni / form.
The neighbor, black face, green head rag, says
"She was a good woman, raising six good children,
They used to play here in the hallway."

WALKING THE STREETS OF MEMPHIS AT 3 A.M., DEAD / BROKE AND STONE / SOBER

The Night feels like wet leaves.
There / is / a mist around me, between me
And the moon. On Jackson street an ambulance
Slings its scream over Baron Hirsch Synagogue.
I think of Nazi Policemen in a Paul Muni movie.
The neighborhood dogs
               howl from the hurt in their ears.
I walk, swinging a rusty golf club and scheming
On tomorrow's
               bread and beer. I have fathered babies.
The first, girl, whose name means —
high yellow, and as sweet molasses.

POETFOLIO

Beyond this green field
Men assault trees, earth —
Build *another* prison — damn!

My lover is gone,
O will she return?
My song is a summer storm...

This peach —
sitting by my typewriter, looks so sweet!
My tongue will soon know.

Fourth of July!
Barbeque... beer... flags... cheer...
Tomorrow, bombs, blood, open graves.

Come! bring breath, body...
On Blue mountain, trees, lakes, — sing!
I dance, day and night.

O Br'er bo' weevils!
Way 'way from Mex'co — eat — eat!
Boss be mad; me, — glad!

Green caterpillar,
Crawling / up / my belly,
Where you from? where you go?

Flower, mountain, sky,
Flowing river, stinging bee —
I am you — you — me!

O black snake,
Wiggling in this lake,
I was once slim and brave too.

Frozen lakes, snowy
Mountains, plenty sky.
O to hear the whippoorwill's cry

Brothers: deer, trees, bear...
O Blue Mountain! when bombers
Slash this bless'd air,
Do your hearts tremble like mine?

SONG OF BR'ER MUD-TURTLE

Ol' Br'er Mud-Turtle was settin on a log,
Watching a lil tadpole aturnin' to a frog;

When he saw Br'er Bear apulling like a mule,
And ol Br'er Terrapin amaking him outta fool.

Br'er Bear apulling on a rope; he puff and he blow;
But he can't git Br'er Terrapin outta the water below.

[SOMEWHERE IN THE FREE]

Somewhere in the free
Waters you splash up with-
Out advance notice……

And you never fail
To blind me with your blackness
Before the great fall

[IF YOU WANT TO FIND GOD]

If you want to find God, look into
your mother's eyes.

A MOTHER'S DAY POEM, 1985

Of all the Women in the World,
I would want none other
                    than you,
Belzora Matilda LouElla Cozart Knight Taylor,
To be my Black, Baptist Mother.
                    Just you.

[OUT OF THE TUNNEL INTO THE MISSISSIPPI SUN]

Out of the tunnel into the Mississippi sun
I have always been a lonely one
A lonely boy playing in the dust and shade,
A lonely brother, overpowered by two others,
encircled by four sisters, and a mother.

MOUNTAIN MOTHER

*Hide nothing from the people, tell no lies,
mask no difficulties... Claim no easy victories.
Our people are our mountains.*

— Amílcar Cabral

The woman rides at my side. The sun sends
shadows over her cheekbones. She stares ahead
and begins to hum a song, lord I want to cross over.
She smells of leaves and bacon and mississippi
nights when guitars could be heard above the shouts
of children catching fireflies in fruit jars.

RIDE, SALLY RIDE

> Lil Sally Walker, sitting in a saucer —
> (Ride, Sally, ride) blink your pretty eyes
>
> — Traditional children's song

The Whirling / is / first.
When the Whirling is done
And you Dance on the rim
Of the world, ride on, girl
When the Fist is unfurled
And the back-slapping ends
Then the hip / shaking begins
In the East and the West
Where the sun sleeps
Like a well-fed child
At her mother's breast.
Blink your eyes, Sally Ride
And the moon will rise
In the sea,
From the wide / open mouth
of me.

Be bold with backbone. Take hold of the time.
Ride. Flying the saucer. Be
The Rime, be the saucy rhythm, be
The hipshaking in the circle,
Always the rhythm, moon — blood singing, always
The cradle and the sea-steady rocking.

You can do it, you can do it.
C'mon, you can do it, Be.

FOR JENIFER McKIM

When I was twenty —
Like you;
I knew a plenty
That's true
And I too
Was full of breath

Now tho, I'm fifty-five,
Alive, and full of jive
And righteous rage
I yet bless the days.
I loathe death.

July 28, 1986

SHE COMES TO ME

(For Bett Gordon)

She comes to me
The Wild Woman bringing
Flowers & music, & *Revolution*
(And Trouble) And
the serious mysteries
And love. And Golden shoes —
            (And the blues)
And circumlocutions
And a Twirling and a Whirling
And a bringing of Breath,
I love her.
To my Death.
Which is a whirling and a twirling
And bringing of Breath.
And my Sisters & Mother Circled
Her in Jubilee.
Yesiree!

PLEA POEM

Hey, Maggie Brown!
               Woman,
What're you putting / down?
I ain't heard one human
Word from you —
What're you trying to do? —
Make this Black Poet blue?

THIS SUN IS HOT

This sun is hot, this hoe is heavy,
This grass grows farther than I can reach;
And as I look at this cotton field —
I think I musta been called to preach!

THE HYPOCRITE

I'll tell you what that hypocrite do:
He comes to my house and talks about you;
He talk about me, and he talk about you;
And that's the way that hypocrite do.

I'll tell you how that hypocrite pray:
He pray out loud in the hypocrite way;
He pray out loud — got a *heap* to say;
And that's the way that hypocrite pray.

I'll tell you how that hypocrite preten':
He preten' that he loves, but he *don't* love men;
How can he love when he hates Br'er Ben?
And that's the way that hypocrite preten'.

OLD MAN KNOW-ALL

Ol man Know-All, he come around
With his nose in the air — turned up from the ground.
His ol wooly head ain't been combed for a week;
It say, "Keep quiet, while Know-All speak."

Ol man Know-All's tongue, it really run;
He knowed about everything under the sun;
When you knowed one thing — he knowed mo';
He sharp enough to stick, and green enough to grow.

Ol man Know-All died last week!
He got drowned in the middle of the creek!
The bridge was there, and there to stay —
But he *knowed* too much to go that way!

REVOLUTIONARIES LIVE IN HOUSES OF LOVE

(For Hank and Wendy Keene-Sanel)

The Sun / Son rises in the East Henry,
Remember Max, in his innocence, and remember
Even when the Glitter of Gold and the Glowing
Of Head when Men (and Women) sing praise to You —
Remember Max, and the sacred OATH of the Healer:
To relieve Pain and Suffering.

Is the Finest, the Primest of all / the / Arts.
Do / NOT / trust the *lineal* lie of Science / Medicine.
The Art of Healing is Feminine, circular, holy.

I sing this poem, preachy and with / out rhyme
Or Reason, I sing of the Love that flows
From your lips and your hippy / dippy New York strut;
Good men walk a / way / that women know
And their nipples harden and their palms
Caress their Bellies that bear the Babies.

O Henry, you / are / a New Father, a New Man,
In a House built of Love, not Fear, the plan
Of Yahweh and Allah and Buddha and Damballa
And Brahma and Jehovah is dead
No matter what / is / said by Jerry Falwell
Or the Pope, or the hope of Khomani,
The Chiefs in the East, or the Boss Rabbi,
Even Jah, the Father of all / Patriarchs

Has become a lie.

You / are / a New Father. I know this is true
By the / way / Wendy looks at you —
Despite the ideological odds and ends,
You / two blend
In a revolutionary Love
That / will create a space for Seth and Max
To live in dignity and graceful communication
With / all / men, women, and children on this earth-nation.

Heal the People, Listen (not submit) to your Woman.
Relieve the suffering and pain.
You is she, and she is Thee.
Amen.

AFTER LISTENING TO ERNESTO CARDENAL

Poetry among the People?
Among the workers, the children, the singers,
And the policeman, bluebirds lighting
On military shoulders.

E. S.

You kept moving, always moving,
From the patchwork quilt on the bed,
To the bathroom, to the bottle
Of Jack Daniels in the kitchen.
I followed you like a shadow
The miracle of your freckles, the curve
Of your back, your calves, your thighs,
The clean-shaven place and your green eyes
Always soft and warm like the flannel
Gown I bought for you on Beale St.

I NEED FOR YOU TO TELL ME

When the sun is sinking low
When on the radio
I hear the sad trumpets blow
And my tears begin to flow
I need for you to say
O I love you.

DEATHROW

"Well, they burned tough Tony last night
The man who didn't know the meaning of fright"

Today's June first, today I go —
Today's my turn / to be / the star of the show
First comes Jojo, then Big Red —
But the main event's over, after I'm dead.
There'll / be / lights, and cameras, — and plenty action —
And ol' Mr. K. the main attraction.
There won't / be / no crying or copping no pleas,
Hanging on the bars or begging on my knees.
When it comes to / me / to walk the last mile —
I'll hold my head high — even wear a smile.

— Traditional (version, EK) June 1, 1983

O ELIZABETH

Woman of my wanderings —
Wife of my comings and goings —
Sister of my rap and rhyme,
I thank thee, goode Giver,
for the gift of Time and Tenderness,
You bless my 58th year, tho
I be / here / in this Domain
of Death and Excellent Pain
I languish. I suffer. I exalt —
Do you still love me? Is —
my smoke still in your
fire? How can you love me?
Me: liar cheater and dirty
mistreater / I love you
I, man of the high step
and the long-laugh.
Despite the rocks and
shoals and silver water
falls, our rivers flow
together. Who knows
what the weather / will
be tomorrow, We row
for sunshine, not storm,
We row for joy not sorrow

CHANCE DANCER

I don't feel
like I got cancer
I feel like a dancer
and tho' there's not much music
what li'l there is
I use it.

THE DANCE

Our Dance, ms. E.,
Is Definite,
And a Dare
To be Free;
A whirl here, a Drag there;
Our Dance takes Us everywhere —
Up this Hill; across that Ridge,
And River, Bells are ringing
"Freedom! C'mon!"

We dance upon the Bridge
Of our / own / true Singing;
And the WE dance
Is the Free dance.

And O Dear D.,
Sister and Brother
We already Be,
Naturally,
By blood, and by Race.
But I desire a Dance
With Thee.
With Thee I sing
The rhythms of the Caribbean
And the lazy Grace
Of Mississippi.
So come dance! Dear D. —
Come dance with WE.

With bells on our ankles,
With flowers in our teeth —
O the WE Dance
Is the Free Dance.

A-B-C!
A-B-C!

By All the Singers
Below, above,
And within Me,

I sing Thee Peace —
I sing the Love —
I sing Thee Free / dom
For WE.
Not One.
I am Done.

prose

PREFACE TO BORN OF A WOMAN

Poets are naturally meddlers. They meddle in other people's lives and they meddle in their own, always searching and loving and questioning and digging into this or that. Poets meddle with whores — they meddle with politicians, zen, the church, god, and children; they meddle with monkeys, freaks, soft warm lovers, flowers, whiskey, dope, and other artists — especially jive-assed doctors. Poets are sometimes prophets and sometimes fakes. Some poets live to meddle for a lloongg time, till their hair is white, like Robert Frost; and some poets meddle only for a moment, like Henry Dumas, shot in the back at twenty-four by one of "New York City's Finest" in a subway station. Some poets meddle big, like Mao, who sang his song to hundreds of millions, and some poets meddle little, like Emily Dickinson, tucking her poems among the cookies that she shared with her neighbors. All poets meddle, in one way or another.

One of the main justifications for a poet's meddling is loving concern. Jesus meddled with people and so did Hitler. A social worker's meddling is somewhat different from those Watergate guys meddling in the office of Daniel Ellsberg's doctor. The result of a poet's meddling emerges in different ways. Sometimes it's a howl or a scream; sometimes it's a love song or a jubilee; and sometimes it's "arty" intellectual masturbation. But always the main motivation must be loving concern, or else it's bullshit.

The poems you are about to read came into being during the past fifteen or so years of meddling. In prison, and outta prison. In pool halls, college campuses, street corners, churches, and city parks. You'll notice that I have made slight changes in some of the "older" poems. A phrase altered here and there, a word added or dropped. The reason is — while reading my poems around the country, I became aware (sometimes I was *made* aware) that I was perpetuating the racism and sexism that is inherent in our language. For instance, an "English" teacher at Bucks County Community College in Pennsylvania pointed out to me, quite firmly, that the line "And we all waited and watched, like indians at a corral" — from "Hard Rock Returns" — contained a racist phrase. And she was right. And so I changed "like indians at a corral" to "like a herd of sheep." In another instance, a young woman poet at the 1975 National Poetry Festival convinced me that the last lines in "The Idea of Ancestry" — "...and I have no sons / to float in the space between" — was sexist. And so I changed "sons" to "children." The list goes on. On the surface, it might look like nitpicking, but actually it's not. The authority, the authenticity, the integrity of the poet's voice is "grounded" in the WORD as connotation, as evocation, as imagination (hence: image), and to perpetuate a lie, an evil, whether through omission or commission is to commit artistic and / or actual suicide.

You'll also notice that most of my poems are about and / or for people. That's because I see the Art of Poetry as the *logos* ("In the beginning was the WORD") as a TRINITY: The Poet, The Poem, and The People. When the three come together, the communion, the communication, the Art happens. That's what I hope will happen with me and you and these poems.

Etheridge Knight
Memphis, Tennessee
September 1979

LEND ME YOUR EAR

A column

I first started this column in the Indiana State Prison in the early sixties. I / was "serving" a 10-25 years sentence for Robbery. And I had / just / been / assigned to the prison newspaper, *The Lakeshore Outlook*, — as reporter, columnist, make / up-layout-man, and token nigger. I worked hard on my first column, stayed / up late / night in my cell, working by the light from my fish tank, — and using all the "big-words" at my command. (Like most people, I / had sensed the power of THE WORD, spoken or written; and I / had reasoned, wrongly, that — the bigger the word — the bigger the power.) And so my first column was / filled with "Whereases," "moreovers," "therefores," and other such bullshit, as "Speaking from a psychological standpoint of view, and taking into consideration all the data computed on the subject, at this point in time" and blah blah blah.

The issue of *The Lakeshore Outlook* with my first column in / it went to press. Soon afterwards, we delivered it thru / out the prison, to the Shops, the Cellhouses, to Solitary Confinement, to the Warden's and Deputy Warden's offices. The task was ended after hundreds of the issue were mailed / out to relatives, friends, and other interested parties to the prison scene. Then I folded my arms behind my head and sat / back, like all / good columnists, to wait for a reaction to "Lend Me Your Ears." And I / got what I was waiting for — craps or natural, or double in spades.

Most of the responses were in verbal ayes or nays and / or palm-slapping from the other inmates as we lined / up in front of the mess-hall for the evening meal. But. Two days later I received a hostile letter from a young / black man, who was then in Solitary Confinement, *"The Hole,"* which caused me to / do a great deal of soul-searching and head-scratching. (A few columns later, I / was to receive a "hate-letter" which I / will get into in a future column; about the racial hatred in prison atmospheres, and James Earl Ray, his escape, and Dr. King's death.) The "hostile-letter" from the young / brother in The Hole said, mainly:

> Dear Brother Tom,
>
> Why should I lend you my motherfucking ear when all you're talking is that kind of crap.... And, anyways, Brother Tom, just who in the fuck are you speaking FOR? And just who in the fuck are you speaking TO?

I / was hurt, and outraged. Just who-in-the-fuck did *he* / think *he* / was, talking to me, a "published poet," like that? Why, hadn't I spent years reading every book I could find that related to Poetry or Creative Writing? And weren't I corresponding with, and being / visited by, some of the best poets and writers in the country, — all of whom described my work as "original" and "brilliant" and blah blah? I raved and I ranted. I'll just ignore the dummy, I told myself, and my friends — it'll / be *his* loss, not *mine*. Yet, the young / man's words hung in my head and belly, until I / admitted that, in spite of his harsh tone, his questions were valid, and deserved an answer, one as honestly and as simply as I could make it — and then, one just as honestly, but then not so / simply. So, like Gwen Brooks' lil Lincoln West, I thunk and I thunk and I / thunk; and this / is what I came / up / with:

> Dear Young Fool, I said (I just / couldn't help being a smart / ass), the questions in your letter have kept me occupied for a couple of days (as you probably intended, having nothing better to do in the hole, other than to masturbate and speculate). Well, first of all, as far as my Poetry goes,

and this column, I / am speaking to, and for, my / own / self, and (2) I / am speaking to and for selves like my / self — and that / is / you, and third, I / am speaking to and for the / other / selves, who / are essentially like you and me, but whose existence is not like / ours. Dig that? Now, to the complications:

THE ONE I / AM SPEAKING TO, AND THE ONE I / AM SPEAKING FOR, ARE PRIMARILY, AND ULTIMATELY, ONE AND THE SAME. (Yeah, I know, but just hold / on.)

As I have just said, I / am speaking first, and foremost, for and to my / own / self — as much as that / is / possible. Of course, *you / know* that one says a poem or writes a column here in prison with the warden's eyeballs hovering / over one's left shoulder, and with the Commissioner of Correction's eyeballs glaring only a few inches / above the warden's, and finally with the Governor's eyeballs hanging like twin light bulbs from the ceiling of the whole prison. Now surely, you've heard stories of the entire *Lakeshore Outlook* staff / being thrown in the hole? — once, it / was / for two typographical errors, and the dude who was editor lost his parole. So, you can see, lil br'er, the main / thang that keeps me from speaking completely to and for my / self is FEAR (know the feeling?). And, while I understand that plain ol fear is the main killer of creativity here in prison (*and* elsewhere), I also understand that there are other killers (read: considerations / interests) like economics, egoisms, ignorances and hatreds, that keep one from speaking exactly for one's own / self. Now, if my words *were* / appearing in the "free world" you could, more than likely, validly, charge me with being involved with *all* the killers I've listed — because, you'd more than likely — find them crawling like worms thru my words.

Secondly, I / am speaking to and for other / selves / like / me — that is, I'm speaking to / *you*. The reality of my / self, and situation, and the reality of your / self and your situation are the same: historically, presently, and experientially. (Sorry 'bout those "big words.") Now take your / self — you / are (me, too) in the most oppressive, enslaving situation in the world — other / than the graveyard (that "free at last" bullshit notwithstanding), because you / are unable to move further than six feet in any direction, and you / are unable to speak, to talk, to any / one, in a real sense. In other, blacker words, brother, you / are uptight. Alone. (And so am / I.) In politics it's called "exile" or "enslavement," in religion, it's called "excommunication" or "punishment," in economics, it's called "bankruptcy" or "being broke(n)."

Did you ever / wonder why a dude in here needs a pass to / go from one Cell-house to the / other? or why the guards make / us disperse if more than three or four of us get to / gether on the "yard?" 'Ever wonder why Blacks in South Africa need a "pass" to / go from one part of a city to the other? or why they / are / not allowed to assemble? peacefully? Same-o, same-o. The ability to move, and to talk, makes for communication, and communication makes for FREEDOM. (By "communication," I mean communion, communing, community — something like / that, — not just the transmitting of data from person A to person B — that's dictating, or dictatorship.) So, talking — or speaking, itself, is just one / part of the communication — listening is the / other. Being alone, you cannot "hear" what / others are saying. But. Back to ourselves, our situations, and our addresses to each / other — and why they are one / and / the / same. I / think you'll agree that "words," or language, spoken or written — *in that order* — are the main vehicle of communication between human / beings. And that words come in / to / being thru human situations and / or realities — and by "common" agreement between two or more persons with these similar historical experiences. For instance, does the phrase "he's a jive screw" evoke the same image / feeling to you and me, and to the Commissioner of Corrections? Does the phrase mean the *same as* "He's an incompetent prison guard?" Does the word "Rape" create the same communication between a man and a woman that it / does between two women? And finally, does "copping some hole" mean the same / thing to you and me, and to Billy Graham? — does it really / mean the same / thang as "a homosexual relationship?" So, you see, young / br'er, you / and / I / are / (here come some big words) — essentially and existentially — one and the same. My / address / is to you and to me, at the same time, and on both the levels I just mentioned. In other words, our / relationship — our communication is both *specific* and *general*.

The third, and last, self that I / am speaking to and for / is / the general, the Other — the essential human / being — "The Universal" — (the most favored phrase of the imperialistic academicians). My / address — and the communication — with the general can only / be created from my / own specific point of departure, which, if valid, must necessarily include common / human essentials: fear, hate, love, war, humor, humility, and blah blah. Take Robert Burns, the Scottish poet — it / is obvious to / me that he was not addressing me, specifically — if he / had / been, he would not have spoken / written in the Scottish dialect. Dig it? It / is primarily thru the essentials that I / am able to relate to him — were / we able to communicate. I could not have gotten to the existential Burns without having gotten to the essential Burns first — yet, some Scots — selves like his / own / self, could come to / gether with him from both points of departure. Dig it, dude, the logic of the belly is back-ass-wards to the logic of the head. You remember that ol / thang 'bout "All men (people) are mortal…?" Well, just flip / it / over, and you have the formula for the Creative Word, for Art… I'm getting tired of this heavy / stuff and am about to cut / you / loose — but let me tell you this: we touched bellies — or else you wouldn't have written me that smart-assed letter. Now, here's what's happening in the joint….

I finished the letter to the young man in Solitary with prison "grapevine" gossip, and personal encouragements to keep on keeping on.

P.S.: After being / out / in "the free world" since 1968, I / have found little reason to change my views about any of the above — except to maybe add a few exclamation marks. — E.K.

ON THE ORAL NATURE OF POETRY

What I want to lay out is how I see poetry as dealing with the oral and physical aspects of language — poetry off the page. My first argument is that there were poets long before there were printing presses; therefore, poetry is primarily oral utterance, and the end of a poem belongs in somebody's ears rather than their eyes. Once this orientation becomes your approach to writing a poem, then the whole process of creation is different because you're making up the poem to be said aloud, to be heard, rather than read. I also see the written word as an extension of the spoken word, not a separate entity. I think it's somewhere about the fourth or fifth grade when we learn to see the written word as a different entity from the spoken. This detracts from our ability to stay in touch with the fact that the spoken word is a physical entity that is as solid as this table and has its own laws.

If it's true that as I'm talking to you bones are moving in your inner ears, I'm physically touching you with my voice.

You know, often you hear that reading and writing goes together, but in poetry I think reading and writing, talking and listening goes together. Often, when we're making up poems we look at the process as delivering an abstraction, concepts, ideas, and we don't use the physical side of the language to touch people, to evoke, because that's how the language should be used in poetry — to evoke. If I'm clear about my fear, then anybody who has also felt fear can say, "I felt like that, too." The circumstances might be different that produced the feeling, but feelings are the same. They're sexless, ageless, colorless. Fear in a nine-year-old is the same as fear in a fifty-nine-year-old.

Another instance of the language as physical is that the rhythms and the rhymes in poetry are very much like the rhythms in music. If you start listening to some music with a strong rhythm, you will find yourself either breathing in that rhythm or moving some part of your body in that rhythm. That's the mechanics of it. The sounds themselves are the basic tools. Some contemporary poets avoid rhymes. To me, that's like a carpenter throwing away a hammer out of his kit. The sounds themselves evoke feelings; that's the way you are touched.

∽

I remember Gwendolyn Brooks when she used to come down to the joint and being critiquing my poems she used to say, "Avoid sibilant sounds at the end of your lines." I didn't understand why until I started getting into this whole question of poetry and sounds in the language. I think it's this: the sibilant sound is hostile to our ears, it rattles those bones the wrong way — sneaky, snaky, slimy. I notice that an audience will start getting on edge if they hear that sibilant sound — too much hissing sound. It's not an idea or a concept that causes their uneasiness; their uneasiness is caused by physical means, by the sounds and vibrations themselves.

In the same manner, there are what I call "glad" sounds and "sad" sounds. If you scan a poem where the mood is lost love or the blues or mourning, you'll find that the dominant sounds in the poem are "oh" and "ah," like "Lenore" and "Nevermore" and "o'er and o'er." And the "glad" sounds are "e" and "i" as in "glee" and "whee." If you're walking down the street and you step in an open manhole cover, you won't say "whee," it just won't come out that way.

Another thing I believe is that language is not only physical, it's a living thing, a living organism. It's informed by the physical environment, by how we breathe and our speech patterns. Therefore, our line-breaths in poems are determined by the physical environment.

We don't speak English. That's a political misnomer. We speak American. This language we speak has been informed by a whole number of people, and the breath patterns of the English are close to the breath patterns of the Japanese. People who live in tight places take in air differently than people who live in wide-open spaces. And how we take in air determines how we vocalize. The English might breathe in iambic pentameters, but we don't take in air like that. I have a friend from Jamaica (her name is Deeta) and she was telling me how they'd be coming down from the mountains going into the marketplace, and they'd call to each other to make plans to meet. "We would oleo to each other," she said. "Oleo?" I said. And it struck me that that's the same sound as yodeling. They would make sounds that would go around hills.

How we inhale when we're caught up in a passion is how our breath-lines come. That's not new. Whitman saw that. Our breath-lines don't go like, "When I was walking down beside the sea." That's not how we take in air. And to force an American poet to breathe in those forms is stifling. That's what I feel.

What I mean by the language being a living organism connects to hearing Donald Hall talk about dead metaphors.

Generally speaking, a people's metaphors and figures of speech will come out of their basic economy. If somebody lives near the ocean and they fish, their language will be full of those metaphors. If people are farmers, they will employ that kind of figure of speech. Metaphors are alive. When they come into being, they are informed by the politics and the sociology and the economy of now. That's how language is. And when we try to use dead metaphors, metaphors that were relevant to Shakespeare's time, then the audience cannot get in because the metaphor is out of the audience's experience. When you're using language to evoke a knowledge that the audience already has, they know it from common experience, and the poet is not lecturing, not handing out data. Gwendolyn Brooks told me, "Poetry is using common language in an uncommon way." And in order to be involved in this creative process of using common language in writing poetry, you have to do a lot of listening. I think one of the reasons Carl Sandburg is out of favor on college campuses is that he's clear, you can understand him.

∽

How we speak in moments of passion is how most poetry is made; it comes almost always naturally in poetry.

America's so big in the first place, the speech patterns are different from region to region. I notice that people in New England will take in air; they'll finish a sentence, "blah, blah, blah," then they'll take in air (a long inward breath). The fact that we can be understood and that the environment of this country is like our region-space derives from the fact that we don't live as close, we have enough space to take in air. For instance, people who live in high places take in air differently from people in low. I'm sure that figures of speech in urban centers like in the North — the live ones — would be different from the live metaphors of the rural deep south. They almost always come out of common, shared experience.

For a long time, I couldn't get to this "timelessness" thing in poetry — you know how people will say, "This poem has stood the test of time?" So, if I took a poem — you know like how the Mormons have their genealogy under the mountain? — well, now, if I took a book of poems and put it under the mountain for 20,000 years — the whole language would have changed by then. I'm convinced that as long as a poem is spoken aloud it's "timeless." Shakespeare will stay alive as long as he's said aloud because then it becomes activity, an act of communication. You know I'm literate. I'm not saying that writing is not important. I'm just trying to put the horse before the cart. I want to put it right. It wasn't until I was in prison that I defined myself as a poet. Then I realized that I had a lot of studying to do. I knew I had to study the craft and the techniques and the history of poetry. At that time, they didn't have "Poets-in-the-Prisons" and "Poets-in-the-Schools." Gwendolyn Brooks and Dudley Randall came down on their own. I had a couple of poems published in the *Negro Digest*, and she wrote and asked me to send her "several" poems. I sent about sixty. I guess she said to herself, "I got to get down and see this guy." Following any discipline, you've got to understand the traditions. It's hard to be innovative if you don't know what you're innovating away from.

But too great an emphasis on the written word in poetry leads to a distance between poet and audience. As I said, I first began to define myself as a poet in prison. Guys in the joint were my first primary audience. I was sending poems to guys in the joint before I started sending them anyplace else. If you can play a guitar or paint or say poems, you have an audience. And you get affirmed. I got a lot of support. Guys thought I functioned like the village scribe. On weekends they would come to me and bring their letters, and I was supposed to be a "poet" so they'd have me write letters to their wives and sweethearts. You got to do a lot of relating if you're going to do that right. You've got to listen. You've got to hear their story. They knew I wouldn't take their business back out into the yard.

I came to poetry from the oral side first. I was always good at playing "the dozens." I used to absolutely slay them. In Black culture, if you talk about another guy's mother or sister and make it rhyme, it's a heavy weapon. You can keep guys off you that way. I learned a lot of poems that we call "toasts." When I was a teenager, I had a mentor. Duty was a wino, and we'd buy him a bottle, and he'd hold forth and say three of four hours of them, and I learned them and wrote them down. "Stagger Lee," the "Signifying Monkey," "The Sinking of the Titanic." All those classical ones. The "rap" songs you hear on the radio nowadays are direct descendants of the "toasts." I have heard stanzas that were lifted — especially of sexual prowess — lifted right out of the toasts. They put electronic rhythm in. These toasts are first rural, they tell stories about animals, for instance. But like the Blues, they moved to urban centers, then other characters come in. There are toasts about junkies and whores and street people, things like that. These "rap" songs are long, narrative poems.

As I said, too great an emphasis on the written word leads to a distance between poet and audience. Then the poet begins to speak in a language that's not relevant to the audience. If you stay too long on the mountaintop, you will miss the development of the language, you will be speaking in dead metaphors, and the people down here will have gone on to something else. You know, by the time language gets into the dictionary, we done moved on to something else.

Another thing I believe is that there are two sides to a word. What I call the masculine, lineal side: the authority for that side of the words comes out of Webster's or the Oxford dictionary. On the connotative side, the feminine side, the authority comes from common agreement. That's the side of the language where nuance and inflection come in; we have to agree that the authority is inside, not outside, us. We have to agree what the lifting of a voice means. If me and you are standing on a corner with someone from another country — Africa or China — and a pretty woman comes by and I say, "mmmmmm-mmm," I don't know if they would get it or not. The nuance is something that the speaker and the listener must agree on. That's more circular and its authority rests on now. It doesn't get its authority from the past; it rests on now, where the language is constantly changing. That's the side the poet deals with. The language of nuance, coloring, tone, not necessarily the literal meaning of the words. Sometimes the major meaning of a word is not even in the literal sense of the word so much as in the rhythms and rhymes.

You can listen to rhyme and rhythms and either feel good or not feel good, just by the sounds. The activity of saying a poem and listening to it is what makes the art. I think that's true of any kind of oratory, and, in a way, that's what poetry is — a stylized form of oratory.

*

My thing about poetry and dead metaphors — let me run this around — is that live poets address the times. I don't have any arguments with dead poets, but I prefer live ones. How can you be affected politically, socially? You can say, "Shakespeare wrote that *Othello*, and therefore he was dealing with racism." That may be true, but only if you're listening to Shakespeare. If it's still in the abstract, you're not being physically touched by the language. What I want to emphasize is life, living. Live metaphor. Living poets. I think it's a valid ambition to want the words you strung together to live on the lips of ordinary people.

(O I hope/all/Thee have learned:
Many fires burn, have burned,
And will burn, bright
In this Black Knight.)

—EK

ON ETHERIDGE KNIGHT

Etheridge Knight called what he did "poeting," as if the sedate verb "writing" couldn't capture the urgency that propelled his work. In his poems, Knight meditates on themes close to his life: family connections, incarceration, and the situation of being an African American man in the United States, who is both desired and feared. [Knight's poems] have a wide emotional range, encompassing defiance, anger, desire, humor, alienation, and regret. In his works, Etheridge Knight fiercely insisted that the experiences of people like him, people mainstream society often ignored or dismissed as "problems," were worthy of being commemorated in poetry.

Knight was born in Corinth, Mississippi in 1931. Along with thousands of other African Americans, Knight's family gradually migrated north as part of the Great Migration. They lived for several years in Kentucky, where Etheridge dropped out of school, enlisted in the Army, and served in the Korean War. He left military service with an honorable discharge and an addiction to drugs that would lead him to crime. By this time his family had moved to Indianapolis. In 1960, he was convicted of robbery and began serving a ten- to twenty-five-year sentence at the Indiana State Prison in Michigan City.

In prison, Etheridge Knight began to write. He later said, "I died in Korea from a shrapnel wound, and narcotics resurrected me. I died in 1960 from a prison sentence, and poetry brought me back to life." His unsparing poems detail the corrupting violence and loneliness of imprisonment. In an interview, he described prison as "a very oppressive, painful, alienating world. You've been, not exiled, you've been in-ziled. You've been cut off from your community (Steven C. Tracy and Etheridge Knight, "A *MELUS* Interview:

Etheridge Knight," *MELUS* 12, no 2, Summer 1985)." Etheridge Knight's writing connected with the world outside prison when his poem "To Dinah Washington" appeared in the *Negro Digest* in 1965. Poets Gwendolyn Brooks and Dudley Randall championed his writing and visited him in prison. Randall also ran Broadside Press, which published Knight's first collection *Poems from Prison* in 1968. A short time later, Etheridge Knight was released on parole.

Etheridge Knight would call Indianapolis home for the rest of his tumultuous life, even though he spent a great deal of time away from the city. He wrote poetry, married three times, traveled throughout the country for readings and fellowships, and struggled with addiction. In 1991, Etheridge Knight died of cancer at the age of 59 and is buried in Crown Hill Cemetery.

Modupe Labode
Curator, Division of Cultural and Community Life
National Museum of American History

INDEX OF POEMS AND PROSE

After Listening to Ernesto Cardenal, 230
After Watching B.B. King on T.V. While Locked in No. 8 Cell, No. 5 Cage of the Bridgeport, Conn., State Jail, 45
April 1975, 94
At Delos, 135
At Forty-four, 39

The Ballad of Betty Dunn, 119
Betty Blues, 209
Beware:, 28
Black Boy, 81
Black Eyes, 60
Black Spring, 59
The Blue Duck, 140
Blues for a Lady in Boston, 202
Bring It Home Blues, 141

Can I, 87
Chance Dancer, 235
Chrysalis, 67
Comes Now the Red Madness, 116
[Coming to you], 168
Congressman Harold Ford, 120
Continuation Blues, 208
A Conversation with Myself, 117
Convict Lust Fantasy, 6
Convict's New Year's Eve Party, 11
Courage, 83
Crazy Pigeon, 23

Curtains for Linesmen, 129

The Dance, 236
Dark Prophesy: I Sing of Shine, 41
A Day in the Desert, 8
Some Days, 203
Dearly / — Beloved / — Mizzee, 190
Deathrow, 233

E. S., 231
End of an Arm, 144

Faith, 93
Fire Circled Rainbows, 61
The Fireman Speaks of Smoke Detectors, 211
First Week in June 1975, 95
For Dan Berrigan, 110
For Eric Dolphy, 52
For Honey, 210
For Huey P. Newton a Blk / Leader, 194
For Jenifer McKim, 222
For P.F.C. Joe Rogers, 29
Four Views, 161
Freedom Chant for Blue Mt. Center, 205
Fresh Snow in Prison Yard, 10
From the Moment (or, Right / at — The Time), 105
Fuck Now / Pay Later, 134

Genocide, 171
[Gush man picks], 71

Haiku 2, 40
Haiku for the Homeless, 192
Hat Questionnaire, 198

Hip / Notes to My / Self, 188
Hippie Girl, 74
Huey, 38
The Hypocrite, 226

I Am a Tree, My Lovers Fly to and From Me, 189
[If you want to find God], 217
The Incantation, 80
I Need for You to Tell Me, 232
Introduction, 157
Iowa Dead, 173
I Remember Minnie, 164
I See No Single Thread, 3
The Isness and the Wasness, 90
[It is a bitch no break], 191
I Try to Touch Your Grief, 148

Jazz Drummer, 48
Jazz Haiku #2, 149
Jazz Haiku #3, 150
Johnny Mathis' Ruby, 4
Junky's Song, 196

Katie Lady — Won't You Please Come Home, 152

The Last Poem, 55
Lately Feeling, 14
Leaving Indiana after X-Mas, 1987, 197
Lend Me Your Ear, 243
Life?, 155
Lightnin' Hopkins Arrives in Detroit, 122
Looking at the Lake Where Otis Redding Lay, 121
Losers, 131
Losses, 146

Lovely Terry, 70
A Love Poem (I do not expect the spirit of Penelope), 25
A Love Poem (And Mary / is / on the High / Way), 54
Love Song, 69
Love Song to Idi Amin, 111

Malcolm, 170
March in a Beanfield, 176
McCoy, 78
Memo #1, 75
Memo #7, 76
Memo #75, 187
A Mother's Day Poem, 1985, 218
Mountain Mother, 220

Naked Boy, 66
New Militant, 62
New York City, 162
A Nickel Bet, 27
The Nixon Flu, 184
No, I Can't Go to Jamaica This Year... I'm Goin to Jail Instead, 147
Notice, 56

O Elizabeth, 234
Old Man Know-All, 227
One Day We Shall All Go Back, 49
On the Oral Nature of Poetry, 249
On the Removal of the Fascist American Right from Power, 182
On the Way to Prison, 12
On Universalism, 26
The Other Side of the Wheel, 84
[Out of the tunnel into the Mississippi sun], 219
Outlaw Sketch, 63

Parts, 142
Peace, 30
People Poem, 44
A Personal Letter to Eldridge Cleaver, 124
Personal Property, 167
Pin Pricks of Loneliness, 137
Plea Poem, 224
A Poem for 3rd World Brothers, 113
A Poem for Lincoln University, 193
A Poem for Our President: Whose Name, Ronald Reagan, Bears the Number of the Beast, 153
A Poem to be Recited, 43
Poetfolio, 213
The Point of the Western Pen, 179
Politics, 169
Portrait of Malcolm X, 31
Prayers of a Prisoner, 165
Preface to *Born of a Woman*, 241
Prelude to a September Storm, 136
Prison Graveyard, 50

Ray Charles' Ruby, 5
The Reading Tour, 163
Rejections, 130
Relaxing in the Charity Ward at Mercy Hospital, 37
Revolutionaries Live in Houses of Love, 228
Ride, Sally Ride, 221
Rufus, 16

The Scholar Envious of His Neighbor, 160
A Shakespearean Sonnet: To a Woman Liberationist, 123
Sharecropping Economics 101, 154
She Comes to Me, 223
Some Days, 207

[Somewhere in the free], 216
Song of Br'er Mud-Turtle, 215
Song of the Homeless, 195
Song to the Great Mother, 156
Sons of Thunder, 151
Spring Star Nectar, 77
Staggering over the Bridge That John Berryman Jumped From, 102
Still Going Strong Blues, 138
The Survivors, 174
Sweethearts in a Mulberry Tree, 24

Terms, 175
Things Awfully Quiet in America, 180
This Poem Is For, 53
This Sun is Hot, 225
Three Haiku, 201
Three Songs, 107
To Dinah Washington, 32
To Gwendolyn Brooks, 33
To Make a Poem in Prison, 22
To Mary Sleeping by Herself with Me Hungrily Watching, 72
To the Man Who Sidled up to Me and Asked: "How Long You in Fer, Buddy?", 21
Truth, 92
Turnpike Landscape, 158

Unseen Definition, 133
Untitled 1, 46
Untitled 2, 47

Vietnam Is Harlem, 88
Vision, 7

Waiting for Trial after Watts, 166

Walking the Streets of Memphis at 3 A.M., Dead / Broke and
 Stone / Sober, 212
Warning, 200
A Watts Mother Mourns While Boiling Beans, 51
Weird Town Anthem, 65
Welcome Home, Andrew Young — I'm / sho / glad that you didn't
 get Hung, 115
What Is Love, 97
What We Make Of It, 159
Who Knows???, 185
Winners, 132
Winter, 64

Yellow Wood, 15
Your Song Ain't Really Blue, 206

The text is Freight, designed
by Joshua Darden and published
through GarageFonts in 2005.
It was inspired
by the "Dutch taste" school
of typeface design.

Darden is the first known
African American typeface designer.

The titles are set in Bodoni.
Considered "prince of typographers,"
Giambattista Bodoni (1740–1813)
was an Italian printer who designed
several modern typefaces.

This book was designed
by Norman Minnick
in late 2021.

www.ingramcontent.com/pod-product-compliance
Lightning Source LLC
Chambersburg PA
CBHW030230100526
44583CB00013BA/665